DRE[illegible]

AND

DETAILS

JIM HAGEMANN SNABE
MIKAEL TROLLE

DREAMS AND DETAILS

REINVENT YOUR BUSINESS AND YOUR LEADERSHIP FROM A POSITION OF STRENGTH

POWERED BY spintype

"Dreams and Details inspires leaders to replace bureaucracy with human creativity and defines a new leadership model for continuous reinvention in a world of relentless change".

Gary Hamel,

Management expert, author and Visiting Professor at London Business School.

"Dreams and Details represents the winning formula of a true leader of consequence. Every student of success should read this masterpiece!"

Bill McDermott,

Chief Executive Officer, SAP SE

"Dreams and Details is a brilliant condensation of both the magic and science of building disruption proof businesses. The book describes how to create the magic of the shared dream that energizes everyone as well as the science behind the details of managing the reinvention of the company. A must read for everyone in charge."

Risto Siilasmaa,

Chairman of the Board of Directors, Nokia Corporation

Dreams and Details – Reinvent your business and your leadership from a position of strength

1. Edition, 1. printing. 2021

Authors: Jim Hagemann Snabe & Mikael Trolle
Book layout: Spintype.com
Cover design: Per-Ole Lind
Translated by: Rikke & Bill Fryman
Printed by: Kindle Direct Publishing
Published with: Spintype.com

Isbn print: 9788771921069
Isbn pdf: 9788771920420
Isbn epub: 9788771920437

Join the dialog about leadership in a rapidly changing digital future:
www.dreamsanddetails.com

CONTENTS

PREFACE

On rare occasions, you meet someone who seems to be from a fundamentally different universe, but from the meeting springs a familiarity, energy and mutual inspiration that is almost magical. This book is a result of such a meeting. A seemingly random encounter between the book's authors – Mikael Trolle and Jim Hagemann Snabe – who have each spent a great deal of time reflecting on how to lead and how to help people grow and perform at a higher level.

Jim comes from the world of business. During Jim's long career at SAP, he saw the German software giant reinvent itself several times, creating new value and new opportunities every time. With his colleague, Bill McDermott, they carried out an extensive and successful reinvention of the company. But what were the crucial ingredients? What made the difference?

> *"For years, I had reflected on leadership. I thought about my mistakes as a leader – and my successes. I had noticed that some companies managed to reinvent themselves while others struggled. I searched for answers to one of the biggest leadership challenges of all: How do you reinvent a company from a position of strength? Along with the inspiration I drew from working with Bill McDermott, I searched for answers from other great leaders in business, sports and art. The British conductor Benjamin Zander, among others, encouraged me to trust human ability and potential."*

Mikael comes from the world of sports. With a background as top volleyball coach for the men's national team in Denmark, as well as

CEO in Volleyball Denmark, Mikael had studied leadership in elite sports for years. As a leadership advisor in the areas of art, research and business, he had the opportunity to compare leadership styles across multiple domains.

> *"My leadership roles and experience from the world of performance psychology led me to ponder the same question as Jim: 'What exactly made my leadership work?' What could I pass on? Just like Jim, I had sought out and studied other successful leaders, especially in sports. Inspired by legendary coaches such as Bill Walsh and basketball icon John Wooden, just to mention a few, I was driven to seek out the foundation of optimal human performance."*

The seemingly random meeting between us was made possible by a mutual friend, Allan Levann. Years earlier, Allan had founded the High Performance Institute, with the goal of helping people and companies to perform better, drawing on techniques and knowledge from art, sports, science and the business world. Allan's ability to bring people together to obtain new insight is unparalleled. So even if our first meeting seemed random, the meeting was probably a natural consequence of living in a time in history with a growing need to reinvent the concept of leadership to unleash human potential.

When we met, a lot of things fell into place, and two worlds united. Although we came from different worlds, we realized that we had arrived at similar answers to key leadership questions: What does it take to stay relevant when conditions change? How do you lead people and organizations to a new level of performance? And most importantly, how do you unleash human potential to enable radical change in a successful organization? Our dialogue evolved as we exchanged experiences and attempted to develop a new leadership model based on human potential.

Since our first meeting, we have researched case studies of transformation and talked to many leaders from the worlds of business, sports, art, research and the military to understand how they led reinvention from a position of strength. Each situation and story is different. However, in all cases, the fundamentals were always the same. All successful reinventions had the same basic starting point for success: human potential, human performance and human desire for achievement and recognition.

Many inspiring meetings laid the groundwork for this book. The process of writing the book was a process of continuous reinvention in itself. Many things were clear from the beginning, but at the same time, there were moments when we had to challenge our own assumptions to come up with the right answers. We are convinced that companies can and must learn to reinvent themselves, not just once, but continuously. We believe that this requires a new leadership approach. A leadership approach relevant for times of radical change and disruption, and designed to reinvent organizations from a position of strength.

It is our hope that the readers of this book not only find inspiration to lead through inspiring dreams and attention to the right details, but also are inspired by the need to do so.

Jim & Mikael

INTRODUCTION

"There is at least one point in the history of any company when you have to change dramatically to rise to the next level of performance. Miss that moment – and you start to decline."

Andrew Grove, 1936-2016. CEO of Intel.

An early morning in March 2014, the season's first race in Formula 1 was broadcasted from Melbourne, Australia. SAP had paid a small fortune to get their logo on two McLaren racing cars, and in one of the cars was an interesting new driver, the Danish rookie Kevin Magnussen.

One and a half hours later, Kevin Magnussen crossed the finish line in third place, an achievement later upgraded to second place because Daniel Ricciardo from the Red Bull team was disqualified.

Excited, Jim wrote a text message to Ron Dennis, the chairman of the McLaren Technology Group at the time: *"Ron, congratulations on a great start of the season. Your ability to spot young talent continues to be world class."* After a few minutes, Ron Dennis responded: *"Jim, thank you for your support. It is a good start, but we should never forget that we are here to win. We still have a lot to do!"*

A classic Ron response. Ron Dennis may be one of the most ambitious leaders in business. He always tries to put himself in a position with the best chances of winning, no matter what he is doing.

It subsequently turned out that Ron Dennis was right. There was much to improve, and McLaren never did better during the 2014 season than Magnussen's second place. Ron Dennis began to reinvent the McLaren Group. He believed that technological developments created new opportunities for the company, and he wanted to take advantage of the company's expertise in Formula 1 and advanced sports cars in an ambitious plan to diversify the group and turn it into a technology leader.

Ron's plan to reinvent the company did, however, meet resistance from the board and the majority of the owners, and he had to abandon it. As a result, he left the company and sold his stake in 2017. It was a difficult decision. For more than 35 years, Ron had helped develop the company. It went from a $3 million company with 70 employees in 1980 to a global company with 3,500 employees, worth more than $3 billion in 2017.

Instead of reinventing the McLaren Group, Ron Dennis started the process of reinventing himself, and today he is involved in reinventing other industries. His ambitions and his leadership philosophy is still impacted by his experiences from Formula 1. As he says, *"The fact that you have won the Formula 1 World Championship many times in past seasons is no guarantee for winning it in the next season."*

The Formula 1 example is relevant to the theme of this book: The ability to reinvent a company and its leadership. In Formula 1, the rules often change radically from season to season. Within a season, the rules in Formula 1 stay the same, allowing only for optimization of cars between each race to increase the chances of winning the next race. But between every season the rules change, sometimes drastically, which forces participating teams to experiment with new technologies, design new cars and engines, rebuild the teams, and above all, find innovative ways of working. Basically, they must reinvent the company for every new season. If you continue to optimize the old car and the old team based on the old rules, you are irrelevant already at the first race in the new season.

That is exactly the dilemma all companies face: to take the risk of reinventing themselves or risk not to? That is what this book is all about – the ability to reinvent a company at the right time and, in doing so, perform radically better when a new season or new market opens up and offers new opportunities.

In sports, it is easy to know when it is time for a new season: the schedule, the results or lack of results, speak for themselves. In a company, it is difficult to know when a new season is emerging, but it is crucial for a company's survival to identify whether it is enough to optimize the existing business, or whether it is time to reinvent it.

But how do you reinvent a company from a position of strength? Most people agree that a change is imminent when results are not forthcoming, or the company is losing money, but at that point it is often too late, since the financial resources to explore new opportunities are limited. The challenge is to reinvent the company for a new season while things are going well, and the company is strong. Change happens so fast today that a company must be able to react long before it is clear that it is necessary.

WRONG ASSUMPTIONS

Industrialization has created opportunities and increased wealth for more than 200 years through the introduction of new technologies, continuous improvement of production processes and optimization of supply chains. We have fine-tuned the way we manage and optimize processes.

It is hard to pinpoint exactly when we went from the industrial age into the digital age, since the change happened gradually, but 1989 was, in many ways, a landmark year. The Berlin Wall fell, and the English scientist Timothy Berners-Lee invented the World Wide Web, which made sharing information on the internet easy for anyone with a computer and an internet connection.

Both the fall of the Wall and the World Wide Web changed the world. The fall of the Wall opened a new avenue for globalization, giving companies access to new markets, new resources and new talents. At the same time, the World Wide Web made the world flatter, as Thomas Friedman writes in his book *The World Is Flat*. It sparked a development that we now are starting to see the effects of everywhere and the speed of change will only increase as digital technology evolves exponentially.

The exponential speed of change is a significant difference between digital development and the Industrial Revolution, which was more linear and thus easier to anticipate and prepare for. Today, change happens so fast that when you start to notice it, it may already be too late to react to it.

If we turn the clock back to 2008, Walmart had a market value of $210 billion, and the internet-startup Amazon was worth $20 billion. Only nine years later, in 2017, Walmart's market valuation was $235 billion. The retailer had a solid increase of its market value, 12 percent in total since 2008. Amazon, however, was worth more than twice as much as Walmart at the end of 2017 and had become one of the most valuable companies in the world. Walmart's value had increased linearly, whereas Amazon's value followed an exponential curve, increasing by astonishing 2,400 percent over the nine years. In the last two years alone, the value of Amazon has doubled. In 2008, Walmart employees were probably not worried about Amazon. Today, it is difficult to imagine that Walmart will come back and take the lead over Amazon. Walmart has started a process of reinventing itself and is now trying to catch up in the new season of the retail industry.

Many companies have had to acknowledge that current success and size does not guarantee long-term survival. According to a study published in the *Harvard Business Review* in April 2014, the average life of the world's largest companies over the past 50 years has decreased from about 60 years to around 18 years. The chance of survival has been radically reduced, even for large and historically successful companies, and that cannot be explained solely by bad management or short-sighted decisions, although it undoubtedly plays a role in some cases. The main reason is that the basic assumption from the industrial era of optimizing for scale is no longer valid. What was good management 50 or even 10 years ago is no longer enough to stay relevant.

When basic assumptions are broken, there is a need to rethink and reinvent the company to fit the new conditions and to adjust assumptions for a new season. The microprocessor in a modern smartphone, for example, would fill up an entire parking space if it was built with 1971 technology, and the mobile phone has more than a thousand times more computing power than all of NASA's computers in 1969 that helped to send people to the moon. And it is more than one million times cheaper. Due to the exponential nature of digital technology, the speed of development in the future will accelerate tremendously.

No industry can avoid the radical changes caused by digital technologies, and reports estimate that between a third and half of all job titles today will be replaced by digital technologies by 2050. It is a new season, and unlike Formula 1, the season change will not happen at fixed times or only once a year. In the future, most companies and leaders will need to constantly consider whether optimization is enough or whether they need radical changes and reinvention. As Andrew Grove, former CEO of Intel, stated already back in 1998, leaders should stay a bit paranoid, feeling that they are constantly persecuted.

We believe that the new digital reality requires a new kind of leadership. One that understands the rules of the digital season, reinvents business from a position of strength, thinks exponentially rather than linearly and develops people to unleash their full potential.

A FOCUS ON PEOPLE

One of the implications of digital development is that jobs that can be automated are likely to disappear. Many classic assembly line jobs are already automated, but artificial intelligence and robots are now challenging jobs that previously required specialized training: doctors, lawyers, translators, financial analysts and investors, just to name a few. In contrast, the jobs that would be harder for digital colleagues to take on are those that require human qualities: creativity, social skills, empathy, intuition and judgment - all of which will be difficult to systematize or be controlled through an algorithm.

This will have a significant influence on how we should act as leaders. In the future, people are even more likely to be hired because of their human qualities. Otherwise, technology can replace them. A leader will need to know how these attributes are cultivated, so the company is able to attract and retain the best talent and realize the full potential of its teams.

Human potential must be cultivated and given room to unfold, not restricted to detailed plans and predefined outcomes measurement. In a time that requires radically different thinking, detailed plans are meaningless and seldom create new opportunities. When people sense a lack of meaning, they lose the ability to motivate themselves and others. Their performance drops right when it is vital that it rises. If management then responds with even more control and measurements, it becomes a downward spiral. In a time when technology challenges old habits, we have a unique opportunity to lead and work in harmony with human nature instead of limiting it. It is a matter of leading in a radically different way with a focus on human potential and human performance. The leaders who understand how to unleash human potential have the keys to unlock the opportunities of digital transformation.

Dreams and Details is our take on how leaders can lead the reinvention of an organization from a position of strength and constantly create new opportunities by focusing on human potential and performance.

We present the background and principles thoroughly in theory and practice throughout the book. The key questions we try to answer are: How do you identify disruption early and react in a decisive way? How do you lead transformation of a company when it is still successful?

How do you inspire people to achieve their full potential and find the best way to reinvent the company to win in the future?

The dream is related to the strategy: Where are the future markets most relevant for your company and how will the company need to reinvent itself in order to maximize the opportunities in the next season? How do you translate the strategy into a dream and an ambition that is able to inspire people to embrace and drive radical change?

The second part of the thinking, the details, is about identifying the few, but critical factors that are essential to achieving the dream. Which new capabilities are necessary to unlock the dream and where do you need the biggest change in order to win in the future? How do you unleash human potential to perform in the next season? And how do you lead the transition from the old to the new season?

Our leadership model Dreams and Details is all about inspiring and developing people, business models and products to create the best opportunities for a successful reinvention of a company. Neither can stand alone. The dream creates the inspiration that fuels the work on the details, and work on the details unleashes human potential to make the dream come true and reinvent the company when the timing is right.

In the first chapters of the book, we will go through why and how the conditions for leadership have changed. We describe how digitalization is changing the fundamentals in all industries. We explain why it is necessary to continually reinvent a company if you want to stay relevant over time. We also explain how a company can recognize the signals that it is time for a season change, even if the company is doing well. We challenge the traditional performance management model with its incessant focus on planning and outcomes measurement. We think this is an outdated management model that discourages companies from undertaking the necessary radical changes and prevents employees from reaching their full potential.

We aim to present the Dreams and Details leadership model concisely. We explain the theoretical background for why you achieve better performance when you set a clear direction, are ambitious and create a framework within which employees are free to find new solutions and develop performance for the next season. We follow up by giving concrete direction on how leaders can initiate changing seasons to reinvent their companies. We explain how to work systematically to challenge assumptions about what a company can do and what the market is. We describe the necessary analytical work behind developing the dream and identifying the few but crucial details that need radical change to make the dream come true. And we examine how a leader should interact and collaborate with stakeholders, including the board, when reinventing a company.

The book also contains our own experiences of leading reinvention of successful organizations. We describe how the reinvention of one of the most successful European software companies, SAP, enabled the company to become the most valuable company in Germany. And we describe how the work with continuous reinvention enabled an elite volleyball team to win 230 games in a row. Our experiences obviously are very different, but the fundamentals are the same, because we both had the opportunity to unleash human potential.

Human performance and potential are key concepts in our leadership model and play a central role throughout the book. Many traditional management models focus on targets, plans and measurement. Targets and plans are defined, and managers work towards fulfilling them. In our view, business plans often limit performance to what was planned. As leaders, we should not limit human performance to fulfill preplanned targets, but instead focus on unfolding human potential and performance in the areas that matter the most. Then the results will follow automatically.

Purpose and ambition also plays a key role in our leadership model. Delivering short term financial results will always be important in business. However, even well-run companies that are managed for short term profits fail to stay relevant when fundamentals are changed in the industry. We argue that companies that are managed according to a meaningful higher purpose, are able to create sustainable success for all stakeholders over time. Purpose driven organizations attract the best talent and achieve higher levels of engagement. They therefore have a higher capacity to re-inventing themselves, independent of size and historical success.

We have written this book because we want to share what we have experienced and what we have learned from great leaders in business, sports and arts. We are convinced that leadership is about inspiring people to achieve ambitious dreams and unleashing human potential to excel in the details that matter the most. We believe it is time to reinvent the organizations we lead and the leadership model we live by.

CHAPTER 1

DO WE STILL BELIEVE THE FUTURE CAN BE PLANNED?

Think back to 2007. Every provincial town had a Blockbuster Video store. At the peak of the chain's popularity, it had almost 60,000 employees in about 9,000 stores in the United States.

If we were to predict the future back then, would we have guessed Blockbuster was facing a new season and would go bankrupt 10 years later, displaced by new digital competitors like Netflix? Probably not. Netflix existed in 2007 but was not seen as a competitor at that time and watching TV on a computer was hardly possible. The speed of the internet was too slow and the new players in the digital market were not competitive. Netflix and similar providers were not taken seriously by the big successful players such as Blockbuster.

Today, we talk a lot about disruption, the idea that new technologies and business models completely out-compete old businesses and approaches. However, the full scope of these changes and the speed by which they happen is often underestimated in big, successful companies. "We are market leaders." "Too big to be threatened by such a small player." "They don't make any money." "The technology is not fully mature yet." "Customers prefer the traditional method," are common explanations.

Everything might seem solid – just like it did for Blockbuster. The bottom line results are fine, market share is often impressive, but the apparent success hides a crisis. Many companies struggle to continue their growth and remain market leaders for long periods. Even the biggest and most successful companies can be disrupted and become irrelevant.

Management does what they have done successfully for decades: create visons, missions, business plans and budgets, set financial targets, define key performance indicators, and look at market shares. They do all the right things, according to what they have learned and what has worked successfully in the past. There has never been more focus on key performance indicators, measurable outcomes; individual worker's assignments have never been described in such detail; and companies have never worked so systematically on optimizing processes.

Those methods have delivered returns year after year in the past. But something has happened. Instead of increasing growth and productivity, many companies experience stagnant growth or even a decline in revenue, and, as a result, they cut costs to protect profits.

Companies are not the only ones experiencing fewer years at the top. The same applies to CEO's, who, on average, cannot expect to lead a company longer than four years today. Despite the efforts and diligence, something is not working. Employees feel less committed when companies struggle and become irrelevant. Management responds by focusing on employee satisfaction and well-being, introducing courses in mindfulness and stress management. It may have a temporary effect, but the feeling that something is fundamentally wrong returns.

It is not the employees or managers at fault. What has changed are the circumstances – the market conditions and customer expectations.

As a manager, our natural solution to the fact that our way of managing does not yield the desired outcomes is often to increase focus on planning and controls. We optimize the tried-and-true methods because we assume that our implementation of them was inadequate. And we hold on to our plans because we assume they help us create positive outcomes. The problem is that plans are often developed based on historic experiences and data and therefore they are only partly relevant for the future. The more uncertain the circumstances seem, the lower we define the ambition level. Otherwise the plans seem unrealistic. As a result, the plans will not create the needed change.

The challenge is that we easily end up optimizing something irrelevant. The methods we learned and used were developed at a time when the future was more predictable, and where change happened slowly, giving us time to adjust. But you can't plan for an unpredictable future, which is why our traditional management methods are less effective and, in many cases, devastating to our ability to react to rapid changes and reinvent the company in time.

When the world changes so radically, "more of the same" will not work in most businesses, and the company may end up like Blockbuster, Kodak, Nokia, and many other former giants – who are either dead or had to go through very tough restructuring efforts to regain relevance. The good news is that it does not have to be like that.

GOODBYE PERFORMANCE MANAGEMENT

New Public Management, NPM, has been declared dead on several occasions, including by the original author of the term, British professor Christopher Hood. The private sector's banner-management process, Performance Management, has also been deemed outdated by several experts in business management in recent years, along with other forms of leadership using the same mindset: The assumption that measuring performance against a perfect plan will ensure the desired outcomes is challenged.

Let's take a look at some of the management practices we have experienced over the years. The Cranet Project is a global research project that examines and evaluates the results of different management methods. The project is the biggest and most comprehensive independent study of management policies and practices in the world. In Denmark, the study has been conducted annually since 1991 by the Copenhagen Business School. They examine organizations with more than 100 employees in both the public and private sectors. The resulting data is unique, as it offers an insight into what methods yield bottom-line results.

In Denmark, for example, formal assessment systems of individual leaders and employees have been used significantly over the past 20 years. However, there is no correlation between a company's results and the use of appraisal systems. The same can be said about many bonus systems and a number of other performance management methods.

According to the Cranet study, there is no evidence that performance management has an effect. Deloitte also surveyed global business leaders in their Global Human Capital Trends 2015 report and found widespread weariness of that kind of leadership. Only eight percent of leaders said that performance management significantly improved results. Another 58 percent said that it is inefficient. According to Deloitte's report, traditional performance management is damaging to employee engagement, alienates the best performers and consumes precious time. This aligns with research conducted by many psychologists the past 10-15 years.

This is one of the reasons that companies like Accenture, Microsoft, Deloitte, General Electric, Adobe and Danske Bank no longer use performance management by itself, but use alternative forms of management systems or try new methods.

We feel confident in concluding that the time is up for management models based on traditional performance management. We still have to measure, follow-up and understand levels of performance and development. But we have to change our focus on outcomes and instead focus on developing human potential. Therefore, it is crucial to understand why it no longer works, why it is necessary to find new leadership methods and how we can reinvent leadership to unleash human potential.

THE INDUSTRIAL REVOLUTION

For 200 years, humankind has benefited from the Industrial Revolution. It has improved our standard of living radically and moved billions of people out of extreme poverty. Aside from occasional local wars, we've seen positive development on all populated continents, albeit at different speeds.

The Industrial Revolution is often characterized by the advent of mass production. Small, expensive and slow handcraft production methods transitioned into standard products produced in large numbers in factories with the lowest marginal costs, often in countries with low wages. It pitted the local carpenter against IKEA; the local shipyard against an industrial facility like South Korean DSME, where three giant Maersk Triple-E ships can be built in parallel.

The introduction of global standards has particularly contributed to boosting productivity. It has made it possible to sell to consumers globally, ship goods far at almost zero costs, and it has created a global market competing on price.

Most of us have learned to lead based on the assumption that competitive advantage is created by producing goods on a mass scale as efficiently as possible. It is a continual balance between price and quality, where all aspects of the supply chain, from raw materials to the final product and logistics, must be optimized.

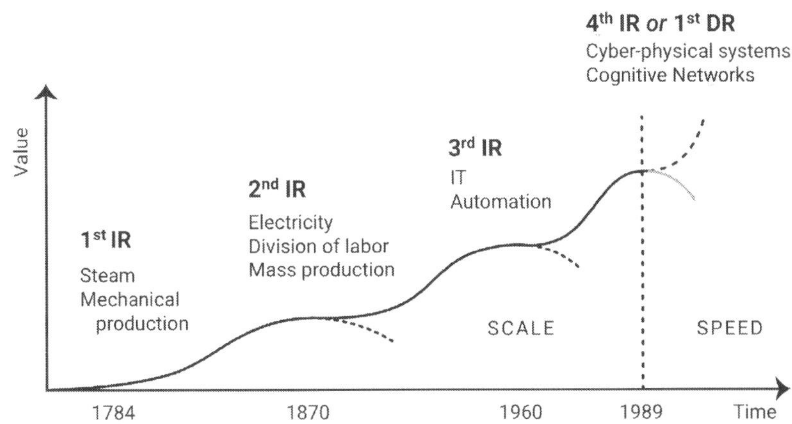

Figure 1: The Industrial Revolutions

We often refer to the Industrial Revolution but in reality, it is more accurate to talk about 'the Industrial Revolutions,' because it has not been a smooth progression. Developments have happened in jumps when new technologies and production methods have created new opportunities for scale and optimization.

The improvements in efficiency and productivity in the first three Industrial Revolutions were driven by a series of trends enabled by technology:

- **Specialization**. Production and supply chains were divided into specific elements, which increased the possibilities for specialization and reduced costs. Individual companies and employees primarily focused on maximizing efficiency in their part of the value chain.
- **Automation using machines**. The introduction of machines made specialized workforces even more efficient; production costs fell while real wages rose in the middle class, resulting in increased demand for mass products.
- **Globalization** and standardization created a wave of offshoring and outsourcing to countries where labor was cheap, especially China and India. Business models were developed based on producing at the lowest possible marginal cost.

Throughout the Industrial Revolution, the supporting logic was Economies of Scale. This logic has created global giants, with size and scale as their competitive advantage. It has been an advantage to be big, and the winning strategy has been to maximize the size and the scalability of the company and its market while minimizing costs.

Looking at the top Fortune 500 companies from the beginning of the 1960s to 1989, when the Berlin Wall fell and the World Wide Web was born, seven out of ten stayed the same: General Motors, Exxon Mobil, Ford Motor, General Electric, Chrysler, Texaco and IBM. This tells us that companies structured around Economies of Scale had a sustainable competitive advantage for 40 years. If we look at the list of companies with the highest value from 1989 to today, it have changed radically. More than 60 percent of the most valuable companies today are digital companies, relatively young, with business models based on digital platforms – not mass produced products.

THE DIGITAL REVOLUTION

So, what has changed? Globalization continues, as does consumption and the opportunity to maximize scale using new technology. Based on that logic, business as well as management models should still be viable. In the meantime, a fourth Industrial Revolution has gained momentum and changed the logic. Where the other Industrial Revolutions have been mechanical, this revolution is digital.

METCALFE'S LAW

Metcalfe's law is attributed to electrical engineer Robert Metcalfe, co-inventor of Ethernet technology. Metcalfe's law states that the value of a telecommunications network is proportional to the square of number of connected users of the system (n^2). In practice this means that each new user in the network – whether digital or human – increases the value of the network. Metcalfe's law is used to explain why digital platforms grow so fast and tend to create 'winner takes all' markets. It demonstrates why companies need to revisit their strategies if they do not include digital platform considerations already. In particular companies with physical products need to consider how a platform can create value and loyalty beyond the product.

Digitalization, in many cases, changes the linear curve to an exponential one, because the technologies are connected, thus constantly gaining new connection points and data, while continually doubling speed, reducing costs and doubling the capacity.

With our mobile devices, we have the internet in our pocket, so we can be connected everywhere to devices all over the world and take advantage of the technological opportunities of digital networks and platforms quickly and cheaply.

Until a few years ago, digital technologies mainly disrupted industries where the physical products could be replaced by digital versions, such as music, film, media, money and advertising. The winners were digital companies like Google, Facebook, Netflix and Spotify, who did not have the disadvantage of a physical supply chain but could reinvent the industry based on digital assumptions.

The traditional assumption that a company needs to own its assets in order to sell its value is also being challenged by the digital business model. Uber, Airbnb and a number of other digital platforms do not own assets. Uber and Lyft do not own cars, Airbnb does not own hotels or properties and the new banking platforms do not have cash or branches. They just connect supply and demand and have changed the conditions for established companies.

Digital platforms transform business models, so the old players that previously benefited from size and scale are overtaken by small but fast digital companies, who know the individual customer better because of their access to customer data and utilization of online technologies to connect supply with demand without an intermediary.

The exceptional feature of digital technology is that it challenges the traditional assumption of Economies of Scale. Instead, the competitive advantage is moved to the platform and the value of the data. Marginal costs and distribution costs of the platform are virtually zero. This means that the earlier industrial-age logic, where competition focuses on scale to reduce marginal costs, is no longer sufficient.

At the same time, digitalization challenges the logic of standardization. Customers are not necessarily eager to consume standard products. They tend to buy standard products if they are cheaper, but most consumers would prefer a customized product if it was available at the same price.

Digitalization allows companies to understand consumer preferences more accurately and deliver on individual needs and preferences. Editor in chief of Wired Magazine, Chris Anderson wrote the book, *The Long Tail*, about how digitalization strengthens individualism. The title of the book is inspired by a graph showing that the aggregated market for niche products far exceeds the market of the most popular products. Earlier phases of the Industrial Revolution favored mainstream products and bestsellers, but digitalization gives companies the advantage to fulfill the customers' exact wishes.

And that is just the beginning. The development has been on its way for decades, but has now gained momentum and speed, as digital technologies begin to exploit artificial intelligence and become interconnected. Through the "Internet of Things" (IoT) most physical products become digitized and connected. Through the addition of artificial intelligence, physical products begin to learn, update and maintain themselves, accelerating technological opportunities beyond anything we have ever seen before.

Chairman and CEO of Softbank, Masayoshi Son, compares this with the biological phenomenon called the Cambrian Explosion more than 500 million years ago, where visual abilities changed our evolution. His 30-year-vision is a world where the artificial computer brain will have an intelligence quotient (IQ) of 10,000, compared with 100 for the average human. The Japanese businessman also predicted that by 2040 there would be an army of 10 billion intelligent robots making human lives easier. A prediction of incredible opportunities – but also many challenges that are currently unsolved.

When these technologies are combined in new ways, many of our current assumptions and business models are challenged. The car of the future will most likely be a self-driving computer, closely connected to other cars, traffic systems and sensors. Sorry, did we say the car of the future? They are already here. Still in the trial stage, they communicate with other cars, computer chips in the streets, lights, Google Maps, homes, calendars – everything we want them to communicate with for a safer, more comfortable ride. Again, not without challenges, but the development is exponential.

Self-driving cars are a good example of how digital development no longer only affects industries where the product can be replaced by a digital version - but all industries. When a car is driving using advanced sensors, artificial intelligence and communicates with traffic systems and other intelligent cars, a major assumption within the car industry is challenged, namely the advantage of owning your own car. When a self-driving car can offer the individual door-to-door transportation and turn the time spent driving into productive time, there is a high probability that many will find greater freedom in not owning a car at all.

Self-driving vehicles become even more attractive because you waste less time in traffic jams since connected self-driving vehicles utilize the roads more efficiently by dynamically optimizing traffic. And if that doesn't convince you, then the fact that you don't have to waste your time finding a parking spot might. Most privately-owned cars today are idle more than 85 percent of the time, a huge waste of resources, so the cost of transportation is reduced radically if resources are utilized more.

Since self-driving cars may give greater individual value and freedom, it is natural to assume that self-driving cars will primarily be offered as a car share arrangement with subscriptions or pay-as-you-go arrangements. For car manufacturers today, it may mean that the demand for cars is likely to decline radically.

Other industries are also affected. How much car insurance do you need on a car that does not have accidents? And who would be insured? The car owner? The passenger? Or is it the manufacturer of the car - or the company providing the intelligent software?

So, as self-driving vehicles reinvent the automotive industry, the traditional car insurance market will also be reinvented. The need for parking spaces will also diminish, since self-driving cars would drive most of the time and only park for repairs or recharging. Imagine the effect it will have on parking garages. Public transportation traffic will probably also be affected. Not to mention driving schools, taxi industry, driver jobs, and gas stations.

The same thought experiment is relevant in all industries. What happens to the energy value chain when energy is extracted from renewable energy sources like sun and wind at significantly lower cost than burning fossil fuels? What happens to consumer product value chains when it is possible to produce individualized products close to the consumer? What happens to manufacturing? What happens to transportation networks? What happens to healthcare systems when we move from curing to prevention?

The irony is that the reinvention of the car, which became the symbol of the second Industrial Revolution and its assembly lines, illustrates just how comprehensive and different the Digital Revolution is. It is poised to make a season change in all industries.

THE EXPONENTIAL CURVE

Intel's founder, Gordon Moore, observed in 1965 that transistor technology developed so quickly that the number of transistors on an integrated circuit would double every year and projected that this would be the case for a decade. Ten years later, he revised his statement to doubling every two years. His prediction was almost accurate. The average doubling rate has been 18 months.

However, Moore was wrong about how long his law would stay relevant. So far, it has been relevant for more than five decades. The standing joke in the digital industry is that the number of people, who predict that Moore's law will soon die, is doubling every 18 months.

Moore's law is important because it describes the exponential speed of development in the digital world. Today there is as much storage capacity in a singing birthday card from the supermarket as was in the computer NASA used to control the Apollo space program landing module in the 1970s. Imagine what that means in terms of new opportunities when computer power is everywhere and almost free.

The American researcher, inventor and author, Ray Kurzweil predicts that our progress will double every 10 years. During the next 90 years, we will see changes corresponding to the last 10,000 years. 10 years later, our progress compared to present times will be equivalent to the last 20,000 years of development.

Exponential growth is not just characteristic of digital technologies, but also human evolution in general, although there are setbacks at times. Just think of the many years we were hunter-gatherers: about 98 percent of human history. When we figured out how to farm, extract and use metals, progress happened fast. The Paleolithic Period, followed by the Neolithic Period, Bronze Age, Iron Age, Medieval Period, Renaissance, Industrialization and digitalization – the epochs have replaced each other at increasing speed.

Human beings also develop rapidly, at least for some time. Just look at a child's development. In a few years, the child goes from being helpless to becoming a competent individual able to solve complicated tasks, with advanced language. We all have the potential for exponential development in us, especially when connected to networks where we can learn from each other and increase each other's performance by training and practicing the right details.

Exponential development does involve a greater risk of not just ending a bit wrong, but a lot, if the direction is not set correctly from the beginning. In spite of time pressures, we should allow ourselves to take a timeout, to use an expression from the sports world, to experiment, learn, adjust and reflect on whether we are doing the right thing and developing in the right direction.

At the same time, exponential development requires us to imagine the future on a large scale. To be aware of the opportunities, knowing that things can change fast. To dare challenge the assumptions that can quickly prove to be wrong.

Let's return to self-driving cars. They have become a reality much faster than predicted. Just a few years ago, experts argued that it would not be possible before 2050. Now the most optimistic predict that it will be a reality in 2020, because the development of artificial intelligence is happening so fast and will accelerate exponentially. Among other things, this is due to the fact that the network of people involved in artificial intelligence is growing exponentially, as does the network of cars learning from each other.

It is time for companies with traditional business models based on customers buying and owning products to develop new business models. Many things will become "on demand." Fifteen years ago, not many were willing to challenge the assumption that Blockbuster was untouchable. Could we have foreseen that development? Yes, and it was foreseen by some. However, it is difficult to accept exponential predictions.

Again, it is important to remember that exponential development is slow in the beginning. Start-up companies do not seem like threats when they are so small that they can barely be noticed. But when they become visible, it can be too late to react. If they develop exponentially, they not only pass you, but also leave players based on linear assumptions far behind in the old season.

That is why it is necessary to be on the lookout for season changes before they happen at scale. You need to know when a season change is on the way and be able to reinvent. The limitations are not likely to be technological, but more likely to be our assumptions, our lack of imagination or ambition and the biggest leadership challenge of all: the challenge of reinventing successful companies.

TO CHALLENGE STRATEGIC ASSUMPTIONS

We have reached the point on the exponential curve where we are forced to challenge existing assumptions that form the basis of our strategies and leadership models. The first assumption that is challenged is "Economies of Scale". As mentioned, the assumptions behind mass production are no longer applicable in the Digital Revolution. It is all about individual relevance and platforms.

The second assumption, that the most attractive markets are ones with the most demand, is also being challenged. Individual products and services have been for the few, but digital technologies make it possible to give customers exactly what they want at a reasonable price. When both assumptions are challenged, new business models will emerge. In order to stay relevant in the future the following strategic assumptions need to be taken into account:

- *Segmentation is dead:* Companies have long thought in terms of target groups and segments. But when we get the opportunity to meet our customers' individual needs, we don't need to think about the most lucrative target groups. Instead, we can focus on how to satisfy each customer individually. This is where big data Artificial Intelligence and the Internet of Things are important because they make it possible for us to better understand the individual needs of customers and to interact with them directly.
- *Platforms replace assets:* Digital technology allows us to shift focus from a product's value to the exponential value of a platform. Airbnb, which provides overnight accommodation as a service, is a good example. Strategically, Airbnb is based on a digital platform bringing people with extra room together with people who need a place to stay, directly. Airbnb doesn't own any rooms themselves, but connects supply and demand, something digital platforms are excellent for. The value here is the platform, not the rooms, and that makes Airbnb a distinctly different business

model than a hotel chain, even though the product is nearly the same.

- *Service models win:* Economies of Scale are being replaced by Economies of Scope, and the benefits of having a wide range and impact. We should not only optimize specific parts of the value chain, but instead reduce complexity and increase impact for the customer across the entire value chain. For instance, a company can go from producing and selling a wind turbine to selling a specified amount of energy from a wind farm. The company is in control of the turbine's operation and maintenance, but also receives all the data from it and can thereby optimize its uptime and reduce maintenance costs. This provides a benefit for the customer and an opportunity for a larger profit margin for the company.

When very basic assumptions are challenged, new opportunities arise that require a company to reinvent itself.

SEASON CHANGE ALL YEAR

The problem with traditional management models is that they focus on executing and measuring what has been planned. Focus is on fulfilling the plan and not on whether the plan is still relevant and makes sense. When companies measure their revenue against a budget, it will give them an understanding of how well they have planned, but not how the market might change and who future competitors will be. An objective of achieving a 15 percent profit margin can be reached by cutting costs, but if done wrong, it could undermine the company's ability to grow in the future.

When we as managers measure individual performance, we measure how the individual or company has completed an assignment. However, that doesn't tell us whether it was the right assignment.

Changes of season will come more often in the future, and leaders have to not only react to them, but actively seek them out as opportunities.

IN SEARCH FOR OPPORTUNITIES

American Professor Rita Gunther McGrath from Columbia University has researched thousands of companies to find which can sustain high economic growth. She has come up with one specific dimension that characterizes companies with sustainable growth: They pursue a long-term perspective on where they want to go, along with an acknowledgement that what they make money on today probably will not be the driving force behind their future growth.

In other words, they are not assuming that they have a business model that is sustainable in the future. They take advantage of their performance now and at the same time are ready to move and change seasons when opportunities arise for growth somewhere else. They typically have a clear direction but not a detailed plan.

When circumstances change constantly and quickly, there is a need for leaders to respond equally fast. Therefore, plans and targets are insufficient as management tools because the plans and targets limit the company to the knowledge and assumptions that were available in a reality that may change before the business plan and its measurements even have been understood by the organization.

At SAP in 2009, success was defined by more than 5,000 targets in the company. The key performance indicators (KPI) were used to measure how different departments were performing against defined business plans. Each department had decided on three to five key performance indicators to describe their contribution to the overall plan for the company. Each department would pay a bonus based on the achievement of the individual targets.

With more than 45,000 employees, perhaps it makes sense that individual employees are held accountable for three to five measurable goals. However, what is the probability that all employees in the company will head in the same direction when they are measured on 5,000 different objectives? How do you ensure that there is sufficient focus on the new opportunities in the next season when most employees are measured using the logic of the old season? How do you avoid a situation in which most individual goals are met, but the company still becomes irrelevant because it is optimizing the past, not reinventing for the future?

If the company does not take action in time when the season changes, performance goals may be met, but the KPIs are increasingly irrelevant and meaningless. Nothing is as demotivating as meaninglessness. If employees cannot see the meaning in their work and the goals defined, uncertainty and apathy arise.

It is important to understand another aspect of digital development: It has made the world more transparent. We can connect instantly, share massive amounts of data constantly, are connected nearly everywhere and can keep up with changes at the same pace in which they happen. This means that employees in a company often have better and more detailed knowledge of customer expectations and new competitors than management.

Traditionally, the big picture was reserved for management, but today employees have access to a lot of very detailed information and, thanks to social media, they can monitor how customers react to products and services. Employees are often the first to notice a change of season, but they may be measured and rewarded not according to their ability to point it out, but to follow the logic in the old season. They may suggest doing something new, but it will often interfere with the performance goals set for themselves and others. In short, employees are limited by how they are measured. This increases the risk of rising meaninglessness and declining motivation and engagement.

SOLVING THE INNOVATORS DILEMMA

In the business world, signs of a season change can be subtle. And if you ask customers, there is never a change of season. Harvard Professor Clayton Christensen writes about this dilemma in his book *The Innovator's Dilemma*, explaining how most companies use all their resources to keep current customers satisfied and develop solutions for the most demanding of them. According to Christensen, companies do not take competition from disruptive starts-ups seriously, and he is not optimistic about companies' abilities to reinvent themselves, because they tend to defend their historic positions instead of challenging them.

We suggest that Clayton Christensen's dilemma is due to the traditional management model of optimizing a successful business instead of reinventing it from a position of strength. There are many examples of companies reinventing themselves and changing seasons convincingly, but it requires leadership and guts to challenge the current success and begin a process of reinvention. Dreams and Details is our proposal to solve Clayton Christensen's *"Innovators dilemma"*.

The lifecycle of a company usually follows what's called a sigmoid curve, named after the Greek letter 'S.' A company is founded, grows, stagnates, declines, and eventually fades and dies or is taken over. As technological development accelerates, it goes faster and faster, making the shelf life of companies shorter in recent decades. By identifying a season change in time, a company can jump to the next sigmoid curve to begin a new development with new opportunities. The optimal time to jump off the curve is when the company is at the top of the curve - before it really starts to decline.

Companies that are good at reinventing themselves can move to the next season again and again. Amazon is an example. Amazon went from being an early online bookstore to an e-commerce platform and on to being a cloud platform, leading the cloud computing season. Today

Amazon is a multifaceted physical and digital company that constantly develops new services and products.

The latest is a digital personal assistant, Amazon Echo. Amazon has managed to change seasons repeatedly – and always from a position of strength – taking advantages of the opportunities of the next season. As a result, Amazon is one of the most valuable companies in the world today. Its value has grown exponentially since the birth of the company.

Season change can also be called an inflection point, a point where the curve turns, as described by Intel's founder, Andrew Grove, in the book *Only the Paranoid Survive*. He explains a strategic inflection point as: *"A time in the life of business when its fundamentals are about to change. That change can mean an opportunity to rise to new heights. But it may just as likely signal the beginning of the end."*

According to Grove a strategic inflection point is a point where critical dimensions in a market change by a factor of 10 or more. As such, it is clear that optimizing based on the rules of the old season will not be sufficient to stay relevant in the next season.

In a later chapter, we will learn more about how to better discover and get the most out of a season change, but in a nutshell, it's about challenging assumptions, and creating a new mindset in a company. It is about constantly looking for the signs of an inflection point and being ready to exploit opportunities in the new season faster than competition.

Andrew Grove concludes that business leaders are not sufficiently paranoid. They may see signs of change and inflection points, but do not respond fast enough and strong enough. Instead, they protect and optimize the old season too long.

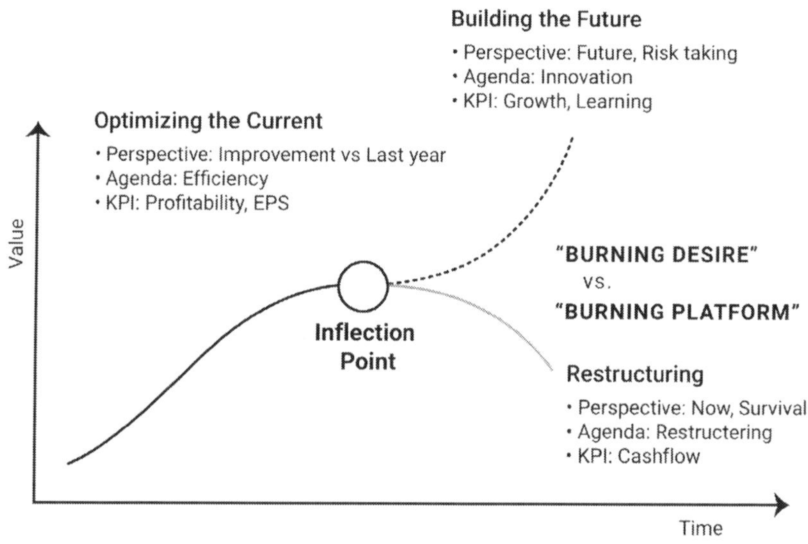

Figure 2: Season Change

In hindsight, Amazon's development may seem logical and natural, but in reality, it is quite difficult to change season while everything is going well. It is easy to overlook the signs that it is about time, possibly because we don't want to see the signs. Most of us have a built-in reluctance to change. The American author and humorist Mark Twain said, *"I'm in favor of progress; it's change I don't like."* This sums up how most of us feel.

In research circles, there is a lot of talk about change bias or innovation bias. Blind spots, in other words. It is much easier to make improvements because they are based on something familiar, while radical changes require new assumptions and habits.

We believe, that solving the Innovators Dilemma requires leaders to realize that radical change from a position of strength is only possible through the creation of a common "burning desire". This turns the transformation of the organization into a positive and opens the door for exploring the opportunities instead of being concerned with a threat.

STRATEGIC INFLECTION POINTS

Intel's legendary chief executive, the late Andrew Grove, is the man behind the strategic inflection point-theory about changes so fundamental that they force a company to reinvent itself or go under. He compared it to the rapids in a raging river that shoot a boat into total chaos and threaten to smash it against a rock or over a waterfall. It is not enough to react to the inflection point with cosmetic structural changes; a comprehensive change of course is needed.

Andrew Grove's formula is based on a tenfold change, meaning that if changes in some critical conditions are a factor of 10 compared to what the company is used to, then it is facing a strategic inflection point. If a computer chip becomes ten times faster, ten times cheaper or ten times smaller – well, then the rules change for the companies using computer chips.

Until now, radical strategic inflection points have primarily hit the digital industry, but today other industries are also affected. The technological development and digitalization of virtually all business areas has changed the rules of the game in all industries.

Grove also noted that strategic inflection points could be influenced by many factors: legislative changes, economic crisis, customer expectations, etc. And those companies ready to recognize and react to the inflection points have better opportunities to stay relevant and survive.

CHAPTER 2

IN SEARCH OF HIDDEN SIGNALS

Our inner reluctance of change makes it even more important to focus attention on signs of a new season.

Even before the last Formula 1 race of the year, drivers and teams are aware that they have to prepare for the next season in which the rules have changed. Other sports do not see the same type of changes from season to season. However, the season change is in itself a reason to stop and consider how we can get better and what needs to change.

In the sports world, it may be necessary to make some crucial changes mid-season. Often you will see a change in the team structure, and you could say that every new game, round or race marks a season change on a small scale. Regardless of the circumstances, the idea of a season change is built into the very fabric of sports.

The same is true for the world of art. In every new theater production, new season of a TV-show, new book or new concert series, the artists are deeply aware that they both have to create something new and stay true to material that the author had in mind and the audience loves. A production of *Romeo and Juliet* should ideally add new nuances to the story we know so well but not be so radically different that we get confused. The young lovers must die in the end. A rock band has to come out with a new album, a new sound, but stay true to their style.

Artists know as well as anyone the requirement for eternal renewal without losing their core. Business leaders can learn a lot from both the world of sports and art, where the season changes are built into their culture. Rarely can we plot the season changes into a schedule or calendar. We have to create a culture in which we recognize the signs that it is time to change seasons quickly and act on the new opportunities.

PROJECTING THE PAST OR IMAGINING THE FUTURE

There are many mechanisms that counteract our ability to successfully carry out a season change. One is our change bias; another is the culture and history of the company. It is more than just a reluctance to change, it is the company's understanding of who they are and what they do. It requires curiosity and courage to go from selling antiques and decorative mussel and oyster shells to becoming one of the leading oil companies like Shell; or go from selling rubber boots to becoming the world's leading mobile phone manufacturer, which happened to Nokia.

Most companies are more likely to build on the existing than to disrupt it. And that makes sense. Most companies should develop their business based on their core competencies, since few can become something they are not.

But all too often we define our core competencies too narrowly. For example, Shell's core competencies were not mussel shells, but the ability to transport products by ship. Shell saw the opportunity to change seasons by paying attention to oil's increasing importance and utilizing their core competence to transport the oil, not in barrels, but tanks.

Conditions in the market can also make it difficult to reinvent a company, even though management has recognized that changes are necessary. As mentioned, Clayton Christensen describes in his book *The Innovator's Dilemma* how large companies failed to reinvent themselves despite the fact that several of them were managed very well and in many cases even saw the change coming.

A large company has to use many resources to keep existing customers satisfied, so it may be difficult to break into new markets. Emerging businesses are typically too small for companies to pursue, since they are insignificant compared to the existing business and may even pose a threat to their existing business model.

New technologies and business models, barely visible, are usually too small in scope or too poor quality to pose a threat. The first smartphones were viewed as advanced toys, not real competitors to Nokia's proven and globally popular mobile phones. But a new market emerged. Microsoft tried to get into that market by purchasing Nokia in 2013, but at that time it was too late. Microsoft tried to acquire a role in the mobile business, but acquired the winner of the previous season, not the new season and not the next season. When Satya Nadella became CEO, he chose to write off the Nokia purchase. It was a $7,6 billion write-off, and more than 7,800 employees were laid off. The write-off was greater than what Microsoft had purchased Nokia for less than two years earlier. However, the decision to write off Nokia was a clear sign of a season change at Microsoft, where Satya Nadella clearly showed his ability to spot a new season and act on it.

As leaders, we know when results do not live up to our expectations. Our response has traditionally been to increase pressure on the organization to make even more precise goals and refine metrics to better control the circumstances. But the result will often be the opposite of what we want: We immobilize the company in the old season instead of driving it forward towards the next season.

Performance targets and budget-oriented management make sense if the future is fairly predictable. But today it rarely is. Even a company with a long-lived, successful product such as Coca-Cola has to constantly consider when it is time for a change of season.

The question is: How do you best spot a new season? Which signs should you be looking for to realize that a season change is happening?

Start with a few simple questions. Which technology are likely to change fundamentals in the industry, and how? When you see a new competitor growing fast and acting differently, ask yourself: Why are they growing so fast? What are they doing differently? What problem are they solving and how is their solution different? If the reason for the high growth is that they are solving a relevant problem in a new way that customers appreciate, it is likely the beginning of a season change. The final question is: Do they provide customers something we cannot? If the answer to the question is "no", then you should ask yourself what it would take for your company to do something similar – but at scale.

THE ART OF DISCOVERING A SEASON CHANGE

When looking for the inflection point as a leader, there is a likelihood that you will face resistance from your company, the company's culture, the market in general, and even yourself. However, by working conscientiously, you will have ample opportunities to spot it.

You can divide the signs of a season change into three levels:

1. Reactive: Crises and visible changes
2. Active: Danger signals under the surface
3. Proactive: Scouting for new seasons

REACTIVE: CRISES AND VISIBLE CHANGES

Lack of growth, a restructuring project, a new CEO recruited from the outside, unexpected competition from new competitors – some changes are visible and clearly require a season change. Often the visible signs of a crisis in a company will lead to an expectation, and even fear among the employees, of profound changes, even if they have not been announced yet.

It is interesting to note that we tend to expect radical changes when a company gets a new CEO. The new CEO is expected to set a new direction within the first 100 days. And in most cases a new CEO will recommend radical changes – otherwise why change the CEO? But why does it take a new CEO for radical changes to occur? As a rule, this type of reactive season change occurs because the company has not reacted to the signals in time or failed to respond adequately to them. Reactive season changes occur based on a burning platform, and in that situation, it is easy to see the need for radical change, but far more difficult to implement it successfully. There are examples of successful reactive season change, such as at IBM, Nokia, and Apple. For all three companies, the situation was so critical that the alternative easily could have been a breakup of the company or bankruptcy.

In most cases, a reactive season change is not successful, and in a future where change is likely to happen even faster, it will be even less successful. A company should not end up in a reactive season change. Granted, some events cannot be foreseen which may change business conditions, but in most cases, the season change should have been seen earlier. The ideal level is level 3: a proactive season change driven by a constant search for new opportunities.

The reactive season change is not only found in the business world, but also in sports, culture and research. It is characterized by stagnating or decreasing performance over time. This often leads to internal fights, focus on individual goals, reduced motivation and lack of engagement. This leads to apathy and frustration, and often the best people seek new and more meaningful opportunities. The only advantage is that the need for radical change is easily understood.

ACTIVE: DANGER SIGNALS BELOW THE SURFACE

At this level, signals are harder to detect, but they are there. Often the company's performance looks healthy. Profitability is fine; the company may even be a market leader in its field. However, if you look at the underlying facts, there will be signs that the relevance-curve has already topped and is on its way down. A season change is imminent. Due to the ongoing digital disruption, many companies probably find themselves at this level right now. The signs include limited growth in revenue for years, or targets met by optimizing the existing business rather than creating new growth. If a company has to cut costs to defend its profits, it may be a sign of a season change. You can not save yourself to greatness.

What does it mean to be a market leader in a market, which is no longer growing and becoming increasingly irrelevant? When Ford started mass producing cars, you could have been the town's most successful horse carriage maker, but it was only a matter of time before your business was irrelevant. A bank can have the highest market share, measured by the number of physical branches, but if the reason is that they have been slower than other banks move to online banking, then they are not a future-oriented business.

You have to look at the market with a wide angle. What it changing? Are customers expecting something new? What is your share of wallet? How much of the customers' total spend within your category of goods and services can you really capture with your offerings? This is different from market share, where you compare your size with competitors. Share of wallet says something about how important you are to the customer. At SAP, our analysis showed that even the most committed customers spent less than 10 percent of their total IT expenses with SAP. In other words, our average customer used 90 to 95 percent of their IT budget on suppliers other than SAP. When this is the case, it is time to reevaluate how you become more relevant for the customer.

It is also important to challenge the usual assumption that a lack of growth is just a sign of a company's cyclical ups and downs. An extraordinary number of companies blamed their downturn in 2008 and 2009 on the financial crisis, and thought it was just a matter of time before things would return to normal. Many overlooked the fact that the crisis masked more fundamental changes, which should have been taken seriously. Many did not recover from that mistake.

At SAP, there was a general consensus that the decline in 2009 was due to the financial crisis. The financial crisis revealed weaknesses in the business model, and had we waited for the former market to come back, we might not have had the opportunity to reinvent the company in time.

Another danger signal can be spotted in employee engagement or lack thereof. During a season change, employees closest to the customers often see the first signs of a new season. They experience an increased imbalance between their customers' expectations and the company's ability to deliver. The result is declining engagement among employees and increased level of dissatisfaction over the conditions in the company.

If meaningful motivation is lacking, external motivational factors such as monetary rewards and bonuses become more dominant. Everyone does what is expected, but not necessarily more than that. This lack of commitment should be seen as a sign that there is a need to investigate if something larger is at stake.

When employees react in this way, it may be because they feel stressed due to restructuring efforts. Often it is because they are increasingly struggling to see the company's direction and relevance.

This is a danger signal that should be taken seriously. Employees often are closer to the customers than top management, because they are in direct contact with them every day.

The company may be more occupied with internal processes and product optimizations than with customers. Performance targets based on detailed plans often will enhance this trend. In other words, if management is predominantly engaged in optimizing the company within the current season, the likelihood that the company, without realizing it, is performing in a shrinking market is high.

PROACTIVE: SCOUTING FOR NEW SEASONS

At this level, the company is actively looking at the market and adjacencies and has a culture that is not only prepared for season changes, but also expects them. It has scouts and explorers sent out to see what opportunities and dangers lie ahead.

Employees report what is happening and propose improvements and new initiatives; ambitions are raised, and new opportunities explored.

The company is also ready to learn from other industries to see if anything can be dramatically changed and improved. If you are a market leader, the likelihood that you can learn from traditional competitors is usually small, but other industries can have valuable experiences that you can learn from to reinvent your own industry.

The mindset at this level is open to optimize the existing business and at the same time be curious about the opportunities to reinvent the business. The company understands the value of having openminded people on the lookout to see what the future might bring and they experiment and learn.

They should also be open to adjacent markets. IBM uses large amounts of ultra clean water to produce electrical circuits and semiconductors. At one point, IBM was so good at keeping track of water sources that it became a competence they could sell to other companies with the same need. Speed is important, but it is worth noting that you don't have to be the first to invent a new solution or technology. There are many examples of companies who were not the first, but were able to scale a new model faster in the market. At SAP, we were not the first to leverage the cloud, Apple was not the first company to make mp3 players, but they quickly saw the opportunities of the emerging technologies dramatically improved the user experience and accelerated the market adoption rate.

Data and employee feedback tells us important things about how our customers act, how we perform, etc., and data can show us potential improvement opportunities and markets on the way up. We can analyze possible scenarios based on data, but the unique possibilities lie in anticipating what the market will demand in three years or even further in the future. Apple's Steve Jobs excelled at this. So did Hasso Plattner at SAP. Intuition, based on facts and scenario planning, plays a role in this too.

Some companies have their own season scouts looking for these possibilities. Others ally themselves with external, innovative startups. For example, several companies, including 60 of the Fortune 500 companies have entered a partnership with the entrepreneurial network, Rainmaking. Rainmaking has experience creating new platforms and services quickly and smoothly and helps companies accelerate their ability to think innovatively and create an entrepreneurial spirit in the company.

Global giants such as Coca-Cola work with small entrepreneurs who have abilities they do not have internally. They do this to challenge Coca-Cola's assumptions. Among other things, this has led to new ways to get Coca-Cola's inventory out to distributors, resulting in greater distributor satisfaction and lower return rates at Coca-Cola.

On the proactive level of season change, companies can also learn from the sports world as a source of development and renewal, both in terms of team performance and individual performance. The coach is constantly in search of small improvements and radical changes that will change the team and increase its chances of winning. They are always striving to improve performance on crucial details and articulate a new dream together as a team. We believe that this singular focus creates meaning for the individual, which encourages motivation, entrepreneurship, and engagement significantly.

FROM ACTIVE TO PROACTIVE

We have found that many companies are currently operating on the active level of discovering a new season. On the surface, things are going decently, maybe even well, but if you take an unprejudiced dive into the leading indicators, the danger signals are clear. In order to take advantage of new opportunities, the company must move from the active to the proactive level. It requires a different way of thinking, a different way of scouting and a more explorative leadership style. In truth, this is not just a matter of a new season, but the ability to constantly reinvent your company and your leadership.

In later chapters, we will explain more about how to handle this as a leader.

CHAPTER 3

DREAMS AND DETAILS – A NEW LEADERSHIP MODEL

On May 25th, 1961, young and newly-elected president, John F. Kennedy, stood before the United Sates Congress and announced that, before the end of the decade, the United States would send a man to the moon and bring him safely back to earth. The following year, on September 12th, 1962, he reiterated it in front of a packed stadium at Rice University in Houston, Texas. *"We choose to go to the moon! We choose to go to the Moon in this decade and do the other things, not because they are easy, but because they are hard; because that goal will serve to organize and measure the best of our energies and skills, because that challenge is one that we are willing to accept, one we are unwilling to postpone, and one we intend to win,"* said Kennedy to thunderous applause.

President Kennedy could have expressed it in many other ways. He could have said that the United States would become the world's leading innovator of technology, surpassing the Soviet Union, and set a number of specific goals, such as the number of patents filed, to achieve it. Would that have seemed inspiring? Probably not.

Kennedy admitted in his speech that a large number of necessary conditions for a lunar landing were not yet present. It required metal alloys and techniques that had not been invented at the time. They gradually did though.

The Space Race was not just about saber rattling. It ushered in an era filled with technological advances and new insights, materials and inventions that today are used far beyond spacecraft: memory foam, insulin pumps, insulation materials, ear thermometers and microchips are just a few. Today, NASA owns thousands of patents, and a myriad of private and public companies have emerged based on the knowledge and technology that space research brought with it. And the United States became a leading technology-producing nation.

Seven years after Kennedy's speech in Houston, Neil Armstrong walked on the face of the moon.

DREAM AND DETAILS – AND THE PLATFORM FOR CHANGE

President Kennedy did what we advocate for in this book: He translated a logical strategy into an inspiring dream. It was extremely ambitious, but not unattainable. It was inspiring, easy to convey and spoke of a future with lots of unknowns and infinite possibilities; a situation that most of today's businesses will recognize. The direction was clear – the road was unpredictable, but Kennedy trusted those involved so much that he left them on their own to determine how to best land a man on the Moon and returning him safely to the Earth again.

In the process of reaching the moon and back, there were details – technologies and human performance – which were absolutely crucial. Due to the time pressure, it was also crucial that everyone worked in the same direction, and the framework made it possible to improvise along the way and seize opportunities that arose. The mindset was that security had to be high. The first moon travelers had to make it back in one piece.

Dreams and Details is our recommended leadership model to enable continuous reinvention based on maximizing human performance. The Dreams and Details leadership model advocates for the importance of inspiring people to drive reinvention based on an ambitious dream that points to the opportunities in the future. It involves focusing on the most crucial details and developing the most critical capabilities that enable the dream to come true. And it includes setting the right mindset and framework to unleash human potential and accelerate the transformation of the organization.

Later in the book, we elaborate on each of these individual elements of the leadership model. This chapter is meant as an overall introduction.

In short, the Dream is what we want to achieve. It is derived from the overall purpose and long term strategy of the organization. A dream sounds elusive, but we chose that word because it indicates the importance of going beyond logic to inspire people to be part of something meaningful and ambitious. For some, leadership has been about setting expectations so low that they can be overachieved. This is the wrong approach if you want to reinvent a company. As leaders we must dare to think big and have ambitious dreams about what the company could become. The dream is developed through a thorough outside-in process to define the role and ambition of the company in future markets. In includes an ambition of how we will succeed in future markets and it translates the ambition into something meaningful and inspiring. The dream defines a relevant direction for the company, but not the plan on how to get there. The dream has to be ambitious enough to inspire the necessary changes and must be so inspiring that it motivates and engages. Direction, ambition and inspiration: That is the dream.

The second part of the model is the Details. The Details define which areas we need to transform and perfect in order to achieve the dream. In other words, the Details define which areas need the biggest change. It is important to emphasize that we are not suggesting to focus on all details, but the few crucial details that need the most radical change to develop the needed capabilities and performance of the organization to achieve the dream.

To connect the Dream and the Details, we need what we call the Platform for change. The Platform includes first of all a common mindset for the organization. The mindset is derived from the Dream and defines what people should have in mind, when they make decisions. As such the mindset enables people in the organization to make the right decisions in line with the strategic priorities. The Platform also includes a common framework for the organization. The framework defines the boundary conditions, structures and rules within which the organization works. The framework allows people to act according to the "rules of the game". In other words, the Platform enables employees to unleash their potential by allowing decentral decision making based on a mindset defining common priorities for decisions and decentral action based on a Framework defining "how we play together".

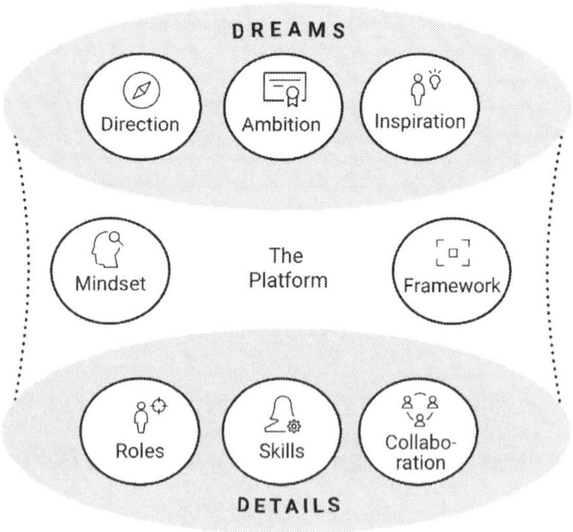

Figure 3: The Dreams and Details leadership model

"DREAM" IS DIRECTION, AMBITION AND INSPIRATION

When we first mentioned our ambition to double the revenue of SAP to a colleague in the IT industry, he warned us: *"The way to survive as a CEO is to deliver more than you promise, so you don't want to promise too much."* The concept of under-promise and over-deliver may ensure a CEO's survival for some time, but it will not enable a reinvention of the company. To reinvent companies, you need to be ambitious. You need an inspiring dream, and the dream needs to have a strategic direction, like Kennedy's dream to put a man on the moon. Where are we going and where do we see opportunities for future growth? How do we ensure that we are relevant in the future?

In our definition of the dream, the dream contains three elements: direction, ambition and inspiration. Direction and ambition speaks to the brain; it sets the strategic priorities for the company. Inspiration speaks to the emotions; it motivates and engages, which is necessary to increase performance, so the dream can be realized.

It is neither ambitious nor inspiring to live by the under-promise and over-deliver rule. What's more, it doesn't set a course for reinvention of the company.

Kennedy said that the United States would send the first human to the moon. That is an inspiring dream with a clear direction. At the same time the dream was very ambitious: "before the end of the decade." You can be skeptical about whether it can be done, but it is clear and comprehensive communication that everyone involved, from the cafeteria assistant to the top engineer, can relate to and be inspired by. It gives direction and meaning in their world when they are part of an overall dream and contributing to it. Meaning is engaging and motivating. Who wouldn't want to be part of a mission to send a man through space to land on the moon and make it back safely again?

THE DREAM IS NOT A PLAN

An important point is that the dream is not to be confused with a business plan. The dream must indicate a direction which ensures that the company is also relevant in the future, but if you want to reinvent your company, we believe that you should refrain from trying to plan exactly how to get there. Planning the path to an ambitious dream will, with high likelihood, limit the outcome to the past experiences of the organization. In times of a season change the future is unknown. So the plan will most likely be wrong. Instead, the company needs to define which capabilities are required to be developed in order for the organization to find the best possible path to the dream.

When Kennedy said that the United States would send a man to the moon and back, there was no detailed plan for how it could be done. But the dream motivated employees to develop the needed capabilities to invent the necessary materials, applications and technology to make it happen.

The advantage of being open to new and better solutions and methods in a company is, among other things that it allows for unexpected ideas and gains along the way. Some of the biggest breakthroughs in the world were not planned but were invented because someone discovered a potential opportunity and dared to deviate from the plan.

As an example, penicillin was discovered when the doctor Alexander Fleming was looking for ways to treat bacterial infections in humans. In 1928, returning from a summer holiday, he discovered a forgotten container with a bacterial culture where a fungus had invaded the container and killed a part of the bacteria culture. He found that the fungus attacking the bacteria contained the substance penicillin. The discovery was obviously based on an unwillingly deviation from his normal research and planned procedure. It was never planned that way – but it was a breakthrough innovation. In 1945, he was awarded with the Nobel Prize for his extraordinary discovery, which has saved so many lives.

THE DREAM HAS TO BE RELEVANT

We argue that a dream needs to be ambitious in order to be motivating. However, it is also important that the dream must be within reach. Like the dream to put a man on the moon, it must fill you with excitement and make you wonder if it is indeed possible. However, it should not seem so unattainable that it is unrealistic. You can formulate an ambition that the Danish men's national team in volleyball will win the World Cup, but if it's completely unrealistic, then it is just a demotivating fantasy. The dream has to be within reach for it to be meaningful.

At the same time, it should be relevant. It doesn't make sense to formulate an ambition for which the company lacks abilities to achieve. An example is the computer company HP, which in 2010 stated that it wanted to become a software company. While it is correct that growth and profitability in software normally is much higher than in hardware, it is very hard to become something you are not. If you don't have the skills to go from hardware to software, it can easily be perceived as an irrelevant dream and won't get the necessary support from the organization.

THE DREAM MUST BE AMBITIOUS

As mentioned, the dream must be so ambitious that it inspires and engages. If you expect excellence and radical change from your organization, make sure you reach for the stars. Companies that aspire to be number one or two in a given market often attract the best people.

If you are a small-town carpenter, your market should be defined differently than if you are IKEA, but the dream should still be ambitious. It may be that you want to be your region's chosen carpenter for built-in shelves, or the most popular local repair man of Rococo chairs.

It depends on the company's skills, but you must define your market and challenge your position in it. If you are the only carpenter in a small town, it is neither ambitious nor inspiring to aim to be the best carpenter in town.

THE DREAM SHOULD ENABLE GROWTH

What do you do if you are an oil company today? You could continue as though nothing has happened, but that may be shortsighted.

The oil business is still profitable, but it is likely that, at some point in the future, renewable energy sources will dominate the market for energy. So the question is: When is the right moment to begin the reinvention of a company to stay relevant in a future where sustainable energy may be in abundance. This does not mean that you cannot make money in the oil business for many years to come, but your dream may need to include other elements already now. Maybe you want to become an energy company instead of an oil company, and lead the transition of the energy market towards renewables.

While there are many ways to deal with this, we believe it is crucial to challenge your own assumptions about where future growth will be and how to make yourself relevant in the next season. Where is the growth and the profit in the future and how can you leverage your strengths in order to differentiate yourself? Where do you need the biggest change?

Grocery retailing is not exactly a niche market, and competition is tough. Nevertheless, the more than 100-year-old Wegmans Food Markets in the USA has managed to gain access to an ever-increasing share of the market, with close to 100 giant supermarkets in the northeastern United States. Wegmans formulated a dream to make a positive difference for customers and their surroundings, and they have differentiated themselves with an ambition to combine an exceptionally high level of service with low prices. The differentiation for their stores is that their food is organic or grown locally. Wegmans demonstrated that it was possible by challenging the classic assumption that high quality cannot be combined with low prices. Wegmans Food Markets is also known for working to reduce food waste, promoting sustainability and contributing to local communities.

Wegmans Food Markets' corporate values state that if the chain has a choice between profit and the health of its customers and community, then it would pick health. As a result, Wegmans has stopped all sales of tobacco.

Wegmans' customers are over-the-moon excited to shop in the family-owned chain, which has been named one of the world's most ethical companies. In a world of tough competitors, often accused of acting cynically, greedy and exploiting their employees, Wegmans stands out as an ethical, but affordable, alternative, which also treats their employees well. The ability to differentiate themselves has secured Wegmans Food Markets a prominent place in one of the world's most competitive markets.

THE DREAM MUST BE MAGNETIC

Wegmans has remarkably high employee retention. Although Wegmans spends more on their employees than, for example, Walmart – hourly wages are significantly higher, and Wegmans offers employees a wide range of benefits such as health insurance and continuing education – the retailer benefits from employees' drive to renew and improve individual supermarkets. And they don't lose money or knowledge associated with replacing employees. Employees stay an average of seven years at Wegmans, as opposed to the industry average of 14 months.

That is a chief characteristic of creating the right dream: It becomes self-recruiting. If the dream is forward thinking, ambitious, relevant and inspiring, and if employees have freedom to innovate and find new and better solutions, then it undoubtedly will draw people who want to engage. As is the case with Wegmans Food Markets, it creates engaged employees, willing to work to make the company even better.

"The thing that bound us together at Apple was the ability to make things that were going to change the world," said Steve Jobs in 1995 on his time at Apple.

Research has found that an employee's engagement and sense of meaning has a clear influence on company performance. Engagement and meaning is also one of the most effective ways to increase growth and profitability. This is found in sports as well, as integrated, personal and meaningful motivation by far outweigh external motivation when it comes to performance in individual and team sports. We will return to this idea in chapter four.

Too many companies paint over the rust, so to speak, when they have a large group of employees who find it difficult to find the meaning of it all. The company creates more wellness initiatives, but that is not where the problem lies. When a large portion of employees are unengaged, then there's something fundamentally wrong, and the company needs to evaluate if its direction is relevant and exciting for employees.

"DETAILS" IS ROLES, SKILLS AND COLLABORATION

The ancient Greek poet, Archilochus wrote the words that the American elite Navy SEALs since have adopted: *"Under pressure, we don't rise to the level of our expectations; we fall to the level of our training."*

This is where the other part of our book title comes in: the details. The dream is a prerequisite for the future of the company, but it can't stand alone. If management designates a strategic direction with corresponding ambition and inspiration, but then leans back and expects it will happen because they said so, it is unlikely that the dream will ever come true.

While working on formulating a dream with direction, ambition and inspiration, leaders should consider what details are crucial for the dream to be realized. The details of the current business are often known and based on best practices. However, in order to reinvent the company, the dream requires that the company is able to perform at a high level in new areas. The list of new capabilities should not contain 20-30 important elements. We are talking two to four indispensable factors. At SAP, we decided to focus on two crucial details, the speed of innovation and the value for customers. In the world of sports, the work with the details is called training. In fact, most of the time in sports is spent on training the crucial details, so the team is ready to win the game. In business, we need to spend more time training the crucial details as well.

The crucial details must be revisited, reviewed and rehearsed continuously to increase performance in future capabilities. Leaders have to look at what roles and skills are needed in the company and how they have to collaborate if the company is to perform at the needed level to achieve the dream.

If everyone knows what their role is, has the right skills and knows how to use them individually and together, they will achieve superior performance needed to achieve the dream.

The first explorers took the same path. They knew which direction they were traveling in – whether their goal was establishing a sea route to India or exploring sub-Saharan Africa. However, they didn't know what they would encounter on the way. Often their maps were limited and sometimes outright wrong. It would have been meaningless to come up with a detailed plan for navigating an almost unknown ocean, where storms, lack of wind, disease and other highly unpredictable events made it necessary to improvise continuously along the way.

The ships were the best possible technology available at the time. The crew was handpicked and trained in navigation, setting the sails, and so on; and their many competencies were tested continuously. The crew understood what was expected. They knew each other and knew how to create the best conditions for fulfilling the dream. In other words, the right roles, skills, and collaboration were present to find new land and handle the small and large challenges that arose along the way.

The solutions could not be predicted in advance. But they had a good idea of what obstacles a ship and crew could encounter and what they would need to reach their goal. The crucial details were identified and rehearsed. The captain and other officers knew when to intervene.

Similarly, management teams should dare to describe a dream, make sure that employees understand it and allow them to pursue the dream. Management must ensure that the necessary roles are brought together, that each employee has the necessary skills and are trained on how to collaborate in a certain way. And management must be ready to take the lead when the situation requires it.

We don't recommend a laissez-faire leadership style, where employees are on their own and can do what they want. It is necessary for leaders to create excitement and clarity around the dream and make it clear which details are crucial. Also, management plays a critical role in ensuring that the necessary skills and capabilities are present and trained, and enable employees to master the details and find the right way towards the dream.

In the following chapters, we will explain how to develop the dream and how to select and work with the details. It is like being modern explorers: the course is clear, we know which crew members should be on the team and which capabilities they need to have. What obstacles are lurking on the way to the destination are unknown, but the challenges can be overcome when we focus and train in the crucial details.

This focus and training in the details will unleash human potential and create high performance organizations able to reinvent themselves.

"PLATFORM" IS MINDSET AND FRAMEWORK

When Louis 'Lou' Gerstner joined IBM as CEO and chairman of the board in 1993, the world expected that he would split up the company and sell it off in pieces. The plan was already laid out by his predecessor, and there was a general consensus that the days of the technology giant as a group were over.

At that time, IBM was in the middle of a serious crisis. More than hundred thousand employees had been laid-off and the company was losing money. In fact, IBM had lost more money in 1992 than any other company in the history of the United States. The reason was an inflection point in computer architecture had shifted the market from centralized mainframe computers to smaller servers and personal computers connected via networks. This fundamental change challenged IBM's core business. Even if IBM was in all the new markets, they struggled to move from the old season to the new. The general assumption was that the best path forward was to split the company up, so each of the individual parts could be optimized and focused.

Louis Gerstner, the first executive in IBM's history to be recruited from the outside, without a background in computers, challenged the assumption. He believed in an integrated IBM and thought that the company could still be relevant. However, he knew it required a radical change in IBM's self-image, which he called inward-looking and inbred. Focus had to move from the product and instead directed towards the customers' needs.

Gerstner launched Operation Bear Hug. Customers were given a big hug, figuratively. Fifty IBM executives were sent out to meet with at least five customers every day, face to face. Their assignment was not to sell anything, but to listen. How did they perceive IBM? What were their issues? How could IBM help them?

It created prompt changes. Top executives' meetings and subsequent reports made the company more focused on customers' needs and how to fulfill them and made employees aware of new business opportunities. Their customers were frustrated over the many new computer technologies that didn't work together. Companies had multiple products from different suppliers, but no one took responsibility for integration.

IBM's management realized the unique competitive edge of being a company with an expertise in connecting technologies and building solutions for customers. If Gerstner had listened to the general assumptions, most likely the conclusion would have been to split the company up in smaller parts, each with its own product category. This would allow each part to compete in the new season, but it would not deliver on the biggest need of the customers. Also it would not differentiate IBM.

Lou Gerstner implemented a new mindset to focus the organization on solving the problems of the customers. In parallel he implemented a new framework within the company. He reorganized the company – moving from independent product units to integrated industry solution units. The heavy and closed hardware business became an open and empathic service business, while preserving the core of its expertise. It was the start of a long period of double-digit profit margins and high growth, where the mindset and framework changed the company's focus from product orientation to customer orientation. IBM's dream to be a service company was enabled by a platform for change including a new mindset and a new framework.

THE MINDSET TRANSFORMS THE DREAM INTO DECISIONS

The mindset in a company reflects what assumptions the company has and what drives decisions. With a vision to create a better everyday life for many people, IKEA is based on a mindset that the price of a product must be as low as possible. The mindset is essential to how employees act every day, as the mindset guides day-to-day decisions and concrete action. What is important? What do I need to prioritize as an employee – price, customers, safety, quality, simplicity or complexity? The mindset decides what to prioritize when in doubt. It guides the individual employee. With the right mindset, an employee can make the right decisions by themselves, without involvement from a manager in most cases. A common mindset is crucial for both the quality and timeliness of decisions and actions.

Often the mindset is not formally recognized or even written down. It is a filter that employees use when making decisions. While older employees may not be conscious of it, new employees experience it very intensely as they try to figure out how to navigate within the company.

A mindset often represents a set of unwritten assumptions upon which an organization's work is based. In sports, the mindset defines how we are going to play the game. But it's not a plan – it's a mutual understanding of how we will play within the framework, implementing and unleashing the details in a way so it is possible to reach the ambition and the dream.

In order to lead a reinvention, we believe it is necessary to change some of a company's biggest assumptions that are not valid in the next season. To do this you need an awareness of the existing mindset of the company – the existing mindset may be an obstacle to change whereas a new mindset could be a catalyst for change. Good intentions based on the dream may collide with the old mindset, if the mindset is not aligned with the dream.

Our experience has shown that it requires strong symbolic actions to change the mindset in a company. An example is the Nordic bank, Danske Bank, which was drastically losing popularity in 2013. The bank was perceived as the elite's bank. Adding to the negative image, they launched a marketing campaign that failed miserably. Their 'new normal – new standards' campaign used the grassroots movement Occupy Wall Street as a symbol that the banking industry needed to change. At the same time, Danske Bank fired employees, closed bank branches, and increased customer fees. The campaign associated with a movement protesting greed in the financial sector contrasted executive decisions and actions.

When Thomas Borgen end of 2013 became the new CEO of Danske Bank, his intention was to transform the bank into a bank for everyone in Denmark, not just the elite. At that time, they had two cafeterias in their Copenhagen headquarters: one for general employees and one specifically for executives. The executives also had chauffeurs. Thomas Borgen abolished both privileges for executives as one of his first decisions.

The change was symbolic, and it was consistent with the dream that Danske Bank was to be a bank for everyone. It showed consistency between what the management said and what they did. It became a signal that management was serious about the intent to challenge the assumption that the bank was only for the elite.

A FRAMEWORK FOR ACTION

With the right mindset, employees are able to make the right decisions, to find the best path towards the dream. However, in order to enable employees to develop and generate high performance, the framework for how the organization works and what is allowed must be well defined. The framework is not just the organizational structure, although organizing the business naturally plays an important role. In the world of sports, the framework is the field we play on or the space in which we develop, train and compete.

If we take the definition from sports and translate it to a company, the framework is, among other things, the organizational structure, governance models, remuneration systems, contracts, working hours, product portfolio, deadlines, economics, etc. These are the elements upon which a company chooses to base their efforts.

Mindset and framework must support and reinforce each other. They are not two separate building blocks in the platform for change, but a bond. The mindset is primarily derived from the dream and enable people to make the right decisions, while the framework relates more to putting the details in play in the right way.

If the mindset is part of the platform that helps us make the right decisions, then the framework is the structure that enables us to carry out the decisions in the best way. It may sound contradictory, but a clear framework can create greater freedom. If you know where the path is, the clarity creates a sense of security since everyone knows what is allowed, and employees can act without fear of taking a wrong step. The framework sets clear boundaries for how the company will take action.

The framework – or the playing field - must be precisely defined so everyone can see where the boundaries or the chalk lines are. The lines can be wide but should not be too wide. Leaders must be ready to involve themselves with those employees who never get chalk on their shirts. And those who do so too often.

The right framework gives the right amount of freedom to allow for creativity in finding the best path towards the dream. Employees have the opportunity to concentrate on practicing, using their skills and working together. Optimal development in a company occurs when everything is calibrated. With the right platform to support the dream and details, employees can bring their full potential into play.

THE RIGHT PLATFORM INCREASES SPEED

It pays off to define the right platform – to create the right mindset and the right framework. It will save a lot of effort to ensure that the company uses its resources where it makes most sense and in the most productive way.

It is possible to have the right dream and focus on the right details without being successful. If the platform is inconsistent with the dream and the details, the connection will be missing, and it may all seem meaningless. You can have an assignment that employees both can and want to solve, but the company's framework counteracts it. At some point, employees will resign or find another place to fulfill their potential.

In business, we have all experienced how a framework can get in the way. At SAP, Jim had an experience that exemplified this perfectly:

At one point, an employee from the design department sent me an email that he had some ideas for a new product that he would like to discuss. We set up a meeting and he brought a mockup of the product. We had a talk and he got some good ideas to improve his product.

Shortly after, another employee came by from the technical department, with an idea for a similar type product. I asked if he had spoken with the employee from the design department. The answer was: "No, he is from a different department." The framework didn't allow for interaction, and because of this, the value from having different skillsets working on the same product were lost.

I changed the playing field they played on: "You guys will work together. You have three weeks. You can use x amount of money – and it is okay if you reach a conclusion that it is not possible." The rest was up to them. The new playing field was clear, and they were challenged beyond their own formal responsibility. However they had clarity and greater freedom to play and better chances of winning.

The framework must support the dream and the work on the details. As a leader, you constantly have to ensure that the playing field is right, so it provides optimal conditions for improving the details and unleashes potential in your organization.

GOODBYE BUSINESS PLAN

Most leaders have all tried to develop business plans to ensure execution of strategy. We suggest that it is better to define the dream, practice the details and define the platform for change.

A business plan allows managers to instruct employees: "You are to do this and that, and here are the results you must achieve within a certain timeframe." If we want to unleash and develop an organization, we should instead say: "This is the dream we all aspire to achieve, this is the playing field you will play on and the players on your team. These are the details you have to become world class at. Please develop your capabilities so you can perform at a much higher level within the details that matter the most". We don't tell what the employee has to do exactly but give them optimal conditions to find the best way themselves.

As a manager, you can give an employee an assignment: "Drive from A to B. The assignment may come with the perfect plan: take exit 42, drive 50 miles per hour all the way and get gas here." It makes total sense, if the traffic conditions are completely predictable all the way. In that case the plan will most likely be the optimal plan. However if the traffic conditions are not predictable, the plan may not be the optimal plan. Therefore it would be better to say: "Drive from A to B as fast as you can without breaking the law. You decide how to do it best." Here there is a clear direction and ambition but at the same time freedom to use one's own abilities and judgement within a well-defined framework. This driver has more freedom to use his or her own competences and is more likely to reach B faster than driver number one – especially if traffic conditions are unpredictable.

In a world that is changing with ever-increasing speed and with many unknowns, there is a need to unleash human creativity to find the best solutions and the best path to fulfilling the dream.

As leaders, the more detailed plans we make, the more defensive we become, because we cannot foresee everything and can only plan based on the boundaries of current knowledge.

Instead, we need to unlock the full potential of everyone in our organization by improving their capabilities within the most critical details and inspire talented people to do their best in order to reach a common dream.

HELLO REINVENTION

In 2003, the Danish Restaurant Noma was founded by chefs Claus Meyer, René Redzepi and Mads Refslund. Their ambition was to create an extraordinary gourmet restaurant. Their inspiration was focused on the ingredients. Their dream was to invent the best food in the world using ingredients only from the Nordic region. The name of the restaurant was inspired by that dream. NOMA is the two first letter of the two words "Nordisk Mad" (Nordic Food) – to remind them of the dream every day.

The restaurant received its first Michelin star two years later, in 2005, and the second Michelin star was awarded in 2007. In 2010, 2011, 2012 and again in 2014 NOMA was named "The Best Restaurant in the World". In record time, NOMA became world famous. People from all over the world wanted to experience the exceptional food at NOMA. With only 45 seats in the restaurant, NOMA was always full and the waiting list was very long.

NOMA had achieved its ambition to become the best restaurant in the world. One of the reasons for this was their ability to constantly improve themselves during the season and reinvent themselves between seasons. Always experimenting, looking for new ingredients, looking for new ways to produce and deliver Nordic food in an absolute extraordinary way, and constantly surprising their guests.

NOMA constantly improved their performance and delivered at an extraordinary high level compared to the expectations of their guests. Driven by the virtuoso leadership of the master chef René Redzepi, the Steve Jobs of the gourmet world, they focused on the crucial details, constantly developing the high performance drivers such as persistence, innovation and perfection. The mindset was totally clear to everybody working there and the framework based on indisputable discipline.

But then something interesting happened in 2015. With a culture of always looking for new ways and new opportunities, NOMA challenged their own success and decided to reinvent themselves from scratch. To the surprise of most people, NOMA decided to close the restaurant at the peak of its success. Instead of scaling the "old" successful restaurant, they decided that it was time to challenge assumptions and learn again.

One of the assumptions they challenged was the assumption that restaurants have a fixed location and guests travel to visit the restaurant. Why not have the restaurant travel to the guests? What could they learn if they applied their unique ability to use local ingredients to locations outside the Nordic countries? They established pop-up restaurants all over the world to be inspired by other food cultures. In 2015, they opened in Tokyo for 5 weeks, in 2016 in Sydney for 10 weeks and, in 2017, in Tulum, Mexico for 7 weeks. They went on an extraordinary journey of discovery and learning around the world.

In parallel, they worked on reinventing the restaurant in Copenhagen. They decided to establish a totally new restaurant in an old maritime warehouse on the old fortifications of Copenhagen. The old building was renovated and combined with new buildings and greenhouses, designed by the famous Danish architect, Bjarke Ingels, from the company BIG.

Noma version 2.0 opened in February 2018. Already before the restaurant reopened the expectations were high. The team exceeded all expectations. Jonathan Gold from the Los Angeles Times wrote: *"The world's most influential restaurant reinvents itself"*. NOMA is no longer just a unique world-class gourmet restaurant. The new dream is to create a food laboratory, or food innovation gallery, that sets new standards in the art of creating food and gourmet experiences.

For 15 years, NOMA mastered all aspects of gourmet cooking. They stayed relevant by constantly reinventing themselves, season after season and as a result they kept winning awards and recognition as the best in the world. In spite of the success – or maybe because of the success – the leaders at NOMA decided to challenge everything to achieve an even bigger dream. Their work on the details made the new dream possible.

The renewal of NOMA is one of the most impressive examples of reinvention from a position of strength. It takes courage to close the most successful restaurant in the world. It takes humbleness to bring NOMA to its guests through pop-up restaurants. It takes curiosity to bring the team on a journey around the world to learn. And it takes big dreams and attention to crucial details to reopen the restaurant three years later – exceeding their own best efforts and reinventing the best restaurant in the world to perform at a new level.

We had the opportunity to visit the reinvented NOMA to celebrate the completion of this book. We could not imagine a better place to celebrate our thoughts on leadership for reinvention. The evening was extraordinary and the visit to the food lab after dinner was very inspiring. The experience confirmed our assumptions that reinvention from a position of strength offers incredible opportunity to stay relevant and beat your best.

CHAPTER 4

THE HUMAN FACTOR – WHY IT WORKS

It was Friday, and the crew of DR TV-Drama's crime series *The Killing* was gathered for an important meeting prior to the first days of filming. The series later became a huge international success, but at this first meeting, the atmosphere was tense. The first episodes were scheduled, and everything had to be ready. Central to the story was a scene in a forest, where a high schooler, Nanna Birk Larsen, is found murdered after being raped.

All the key personnel behind the production's primary functions were at the meeting. The producer, principal screenwriter, director, production designer and videographer, the very best in the industry within their field, met to align expectations with management before the filming started. Everyone contributed by telling how they saw the final result, and how they would formulate and clarify the series' premise. The visual expression, light, color, sound and music all had to be coordinated according to the series' premise and storyline.

The Danish television station, DR TV-Drama calls these gatherings "Paramount Meetings" – using a word that defines something of crucial importance and, not coincidentally, also contains the word for mountaintop.

And that was just how they wanted the meeting prior to the filming of *The Killing* to be viewed: as a meeting of highest importance, on top of a mountain, where the crew could view the landscape central to the filming of individual episodes of a television series. What obstacles were visible in the horizon? What could be hidden in the valleys in the shadow of the mountain? What would they need during their journey?

The film production was not planned in all details. Rather, the big picture was drawn up, so it was up to the crew to make it work and adjust along the way.

It was a demanding approach. The actors didn't know who the murderer was, the episodes were written from one episode to the next. This was different from the normal procedure in producing an international television series, and a big challenge for all involved, creating a totally new level of television production. But it gave those involved freedom to improvise and come up with suggestions to how the story and scenes could be approached.

The approach requires great confidence in the rest of the crew and an overall understanding of the dream: What experience do we want to give the viewers when they tune into our drama series?

The paramount meetings were designed to ensure that everyone was aware of their role, and at the same time had an understanding of the other crew members' contribution and biggest challenges. Everyone was asked what they saw as the biggest challenges of the project.

As everyone spoke during the meeting, an increasing sense of team spirit and direction spread, as well as an understanding for the whole. Here is the framework we work by, the roles and skills that we each bring with us. This is what we are about to achieve. And this is how we need to work together to do it: by having confidence in the team and strengthening our collaboration together.

Each individual knew what the others needed and what their concerns were. Now they needed to get started.

Part of the success of DR TV-Drama's drama series is undoubtedly that they are conscious of working with a shared vision. It starts with a dream that is quickly shared with the producer and the director, who have a major impact on the final results, along with the main videographer. DR TV-Drama has deliberately worked on how to manage something as chaotic as a production of a drama series that begins with few people in the production and snowballs into 1,000 people, and finally ends up with a few people doing the important final editing.

Although much can be planned, there are always unknowns. That is why productions have to be tightly managed – the framework is fixed, and executives are willing to drop a show if it is not convincing after the pilot episodes. Therefore, regular follow-ups and adjustments are necessary. On the other hand, management has to loosen control, to give freedom for the individual and team to find the best solutions along the way. It is said that a script is written three times. Once by the screenwriters, again when it is filmed and finally when it is edited. That applies to every production.

At the same time, each individual has a major influence on his or her own role and freedom to improvise to improve actors' lines or plot points during the process. But it requires trust, transparency and openness to the unexpected and to new ways of doing things.

One of DR TV-Drama's trademarks is delegation. Work is based on trust. Trust in one's own ability to gather the best people for the task and trust in the crew's ambitions to create something unique and outstanding.

The human factor is crucial. Too many internal conflicts, doubts about the direction because team members do not understand or respect each other's roles, needs or concerns could mean that the end result will not be of high quality, and production costs may increase significantly.

If we translate the production of *The Killing* to our terminology, the dream is to create a drama piece so effective that viewers want to be part of it week after week. The ambition is to capture the audience not just in Denmark, but internationally. The drama series must not feel like something they have seen many times before. The inspiration is to open many other layers in the story than just the crime, and to tell an even bigger story about people and about our society. The details are the roles, both the actors' and the film crew's, meaning their skills and capacity to work together.

The platform is partly the mindset of allowing for improvised solutions to strengthen the storyline, even if it deviates from the original manuscript. And partly the framework: the tight management of budget, the paramount meetings, the deadlines and the technical equipment, etc.

Business leaders could learn from the leadership used in high performing artistic environments. They constantly work on developing the potential of the individual and at the same time create an environment for creativity and collaboration where magical moments are likely to occur. That is the kind of leadership needed for companies looking to reinvent themselves.

THE NEW REQUIREMENTS

Many aspects of work conditions in the Industrial Era went against human nature. It goes against human nature to work at monotonous tasks day in and out.

Digitalization is changing all that. If a machine can do a certain task, it will sooner or later replace the human doing that job. If we believe in the exponential nature of the digital development, the automation of jobs is likely to happen sooner, in particular for all routine oriented jobs. The development of artificial intelligence will accelerate this tendency.

Artificial intelligence still has difficulty replacing humans in areas where negotiation skills, care, empathy and creativity is needed. These are unique human traits that will become increasingly important in the future job market. At work, humans are not just a resource; their mind and soul makes the difference. This is a unique opportunity but at the same time it demands a different role of management. We have to create a leadership model that can unleash human potential as a differentiating factor.

Due to the increased transparency in a digital world, employees have a completely different starting point for determining if their work is meaningless or if the requirements that they have to meet have become irrelevant.

This will increasingly make employees challenge the old system, either by quitting or becoming demotivated. Many employees relate their demotivation to stress and unreasonable work requirements or being busy, but in reality, the problem often stems from the employee feeling that the system hamper their optimal effort instead of promoting it. Let's return to the example mentioned earlier. You ask an employee to drive from A to B. Management can plan the route in advance: all exits, the exact speed, the time, including visits to gas stations, etc. The manager would also define performance goals for where the employee should be at certain times. To ensure the plan is executed, the manager would call the employee every 15 minutes to check where he or she was.

Such an approach would quickly frustrate the employee. In particular if the traffic conditions are challenging. Accidents may occur, making it more sensible to choose another exit than the one planned; or there might be a chance to speed up on some stretches or a line at the gas station. The employee will find that the detailed plan for how he or she needs to get to B is meaningless because it was created at a desk without considering how traffic really is. A deviation from the original plan may result in the manager attempting to control even more by calling the employee more frequently to check in, which would just distract the employee.

Alternatively, the leader can clearly express a dream where the employee is going, as well as train the employee in the three details essential to reach the dream: the ability to read traffic, the ability to read a map or use a GPS, and the ability to drive a car. Finally, the leader would let the employee use his or her skills optimally to reach the destination without planning the route.

The mindset will help the employee make the right decisions along the way. If the company's mindset is safety first, then the employee will always prioritize a safe route, but if the mindset is about speed, the employee will prioritize a fastest route. The traffic rules form the framework for the trip.

In this simplified example, you can either plan a detailed route in advance, or enhance the driver's abilities to perform under the conditions that arise during the trip. The latter approach is more likely to be successful if the traffic conditions are unknown. A direction and framework must be present, but the leader's most important job is to ensure that every employee has the necessary skills and competencies in the most critical areas and are able to use them along the way within the defined framework.

The example of finding the way can also be illustrated by another classic management exercise, often used during leadership training. The participants are split up in four groups. Two management groups and two employee groups. The employees are placed on a big chess board and act as chess pieces. The management teams are placed far away from the employees, and based on the game's goal and limitations, they have to decide where to move the employees on the chessboard. A middle manager runs between the management and employees to give instructions to employees and report the status of the game to management.

In most cases, the management team will try to define all the moves that the employees must make. The challenge is that it is impossible to predict the opponent's moves. Therefore, the plan is constantly changed. After some time, the employees lose interest in the game. They do not understand the overall strategy and are simply just moved around on the board in a way that does not make sense to them.

It usually takes some time before the management team realizes that the best way to win is to share their knowledge: to explain to the employees the goal and limitations of the game. When that happens, the employees feel motivated to play, make own decisions based on the circumstances and increase the ability to win the game. The management team's challenge is then that they will feel a loss of control. But they win. It requires the abandonment of control and a strong faith in the abilities of the employees to win the game.

THE MAGIC OF HUMAN COLLABORATION

The type of leadership we are recommending in order to reinvent a company is not new. Our example from DR TV-Drama is based on the same philosophy and approach used in many other creative workplaces. The approach is traditionally used in organizations based on human creativity where the outcome or product is impossible to plan upfront. As a result, the leadership model allows for creativity along the way. Our assertion is that organizations in a changing season also need creativity along the way because the future is unknown.

Kennedy's vision to send a man to the moon is another good example. The assignment was nearly impossible. It had never been done before, and it could only succeed if all the greatest minds within science and technology were put into play to find new solutions. A large number of people from private companies, universities and research institutes were brought onto the project. The staff hired for the space program grew tenfold from 36,500 in 1960 to 376,700 in 1965. NASA had to find new ways to organize how they worked and collaborated, while at the same time allowing flexibility and creativity.

"It may turn out that [the space program's] most valuable spin-off of all will be human rather than technological," wrote The American Association for the Advancement of Science in their magazine *Science* in November 1968, referring to the knowledge gained in leadership and organization that the project developed.

The conditions that NASA worked under during the Apollo program is and will be the reality for many companies: a clear direction and ambition but an uncertain road, with solutions that have not yet been invented. This, combined with the need for quick progress, a diverse group of employees and a high number of external project staff, required a different leadership approach.

Imagine if NASA had instead created a massive spreadsheet with all the detailed plans and measurements. The moon would probably still remain untouched by humans today. Because what use are detailed plans, when you do not know how to reach the goal? And how would teams and departments meet each other's needs if they were bound to specific and perhaps irrelevant goals and judged solely on them?

It was crucially important to make sure that the dream was clear and understood by everyone.

The leadership challenge was to ensure that the needed capabilities could be developed, and the employees could collaborate to find solutions to challenges and adapt to new situations and solve problems as they arose.

We know this type of leadership from the sports world as well. Sometimes a performance can go from being normal to sublime. You experience a team playing together in a way that seems as if every player is equipped with an intuitive sense of the game. Players move perfectly for plays, predict their opponent's moves, pass accurately – every play works and the game moves to a higher level. Those games are exciting to watch and even more exciting to participate in. It is rare that you can play like that for a whole match, but there is an almost magical feeling of teamwork while it lasts.

This level of performance is only possible if the training prior to the game has been focused on developing the players: their technical level in specific areas, ability to read the game and play as a team. Details have been trained over and over again, so the team is able to play according to the overall game strategy.

The difference comes from understanding and reading the game – the mindset of it – not just playing the game. Once the game has started, the coach can no longer call the plays according to a plan. It is up to the team to make it work.

A company is not a TV series or a sports team, but leaders in business can learn a lot from that mindset in order to develop high performance in times where the future is hard to plan.

THE LEADER'S ROLE

As mentioned, we do not advocate for leaders dreaming about a future and letting employees work on their own. Later we will look at how leadership styles have consequences for how an organization develops, but our main message is that leaders must avoid micro-managing and control, and instead focus on developing human potential in a direction that fulfills the dream. Or as the American bestseller and business writer, Seth Godin, writes: *"Leadership is the art of giving people a platform for spreading ideas that work."*

It is a demanding discipline that requires an understanding of how people react, what motivates, and what the optimal conditions are for progress and performance.

Returning once more to sports terminology, a leader's job is to formulate an inspiring ambition and, through optimal game comprehension and training, ensure that the details are in place to ensure the highest possible performance. As an elite coach, you don't have to be the best player on the field, but you must be able to fully understand the game to identify the opportunities and see what may be needed to fulfill the dream. As leaders in SAP, we didn't have to be able to code the software, but we needed to know what the individual employee groups were doing, and what was required to perform well to develop the software that unlocks the dream.

It is not so much about giving the right answers as it is about asking the right questions to the right people and intervening at the right times. Dreams and Details recommends that leaders are both hands off, so employees are free to find solutions themselves – and at the same time more involved in the critical details when it comes to identifying what capabilities are needed and where change is required. The leader's primary job is to stay focused on the important details, and to make sure that employees act within an optimal framework and with the right mindset of the company.

In these cases, it will be easy to set the employees free, and at the same time have the optimal control of the direction as the team unfolds their potential. We are not controlling according to a predefined plan, but we control the way the performance of the team unfolds. This is how you change employees' motivation from meaningless externally regulated motivation to personal, integrated meaning-driven motivation.

Most management books will recommend that leaders avoid micro-managing their teams. We don't recommend micro-management either, although it may at times seem similar. We think leaders need to engage in the crucial details to ensure that they are developed optimally. Not all details, only those crucial for pursuing the dream and ensuring that the company can transform at the speed necessary. We call it Micro-leadership. Micro-leadership focuses on the crucial details that need the biggest change in order to reinvent the company. Radical change only happens when executives are willing and able to lead the transformation of a few but decisive details.

REWARDS AND EMPLOYEE DEVELOPMENT

During the industrial era, rewards and bonuses have helped create a sense of meaning at work that might otherwise seem trivial. The work has not been motivating in itself, but the reward systems have to some extent compensated for this. It is still a widespread assumption that reward systems motivate and increase a company's performance, although as discussed, many studies have shown that bonus schemes and the like merely create a temporary change in employees' work pattern. They do not ensure a change in attitudes to job assignments or a greater connection to the company, more loyalty or greater levels of engagement.

This may seem contrary to human nature. Who would not want a higher wage, or a high bonus?

According to several studies, these types of rewards do not have a significant effect on productivity. This is partly due to the fact that externally regulated motivational factors such as rewards and punishment are not as strong as when we are driven by integrated meaning-driven motivation in which the purpose at times feels more like a calling than work. That kind of integrated motivation is an extraordinarily strong motivator, as it is based on basic human psychological needs, such as acknowledgement of competence, autonomy and relatedness.

Studies have shown that while money is necessary, and we do go to work to make money, it is actually not a very big motivational factor once we have achieved a certain level of wealth. For most employees, it is prestige and recognition that are motivating factors, and not salary in itself.

In addition, punishment and reward are two sides of the same coin. Most managers acknowledge that punishment is a bad management tool. As a manager, it is possible to create behavioral changes with punishment systems, but motivation does not increase, and it will quickly become difficult to keep the best employees, who don't put up with negative behavioral regulations. Rewards have a positive effect in the short term, but they work like this: employees' behavior is controlled but there may be a sense of punishment if you are awarded less than last year or less than your colleagues.

At the same time, reward systems can undermine the relationship between colleagues and they often don't take into account that employees' conditions for obtaining a reward can differ. An advertising sales representative in a growing market will naturally achieve a better result than one in a tough market, where there might be a drop in advertising prices or volume. When a reward system does not correspond with the actual assessment of the performance because it only reflects the result, the employee or the player will consider it as unfair and become frustrated.

Reward systems are often linked to specific KPIs based on annual plans and performance targets that promote defensive behavior.

Employees are not rewarded for innovative thinking; they are rewarded for fulfilling goals that when it comes down to it, could be outdated.

And these are just some of the issues. But if you can't use a monetary reward to develop employees' performance, then what will it take?

There is a positive connection between motivation and having a clear purpose at work, a meaningful role, an understanding of how the role contributes to achieving the overall dream, help to develop abilities and competencies and, most importantly, a feeling of recognition and development.

As humans, we are motivated by being part of a greater purpose. The mission to send the first man to the moon had a greater purpose that inspired people everywhere. More down to earth, literally, one can say it is the difference between selling mobile phones versus "Connecting People" with each other.

If you can see the direction, understand the ambition and feel lifted by it, then it will be inspiring and motivating in itself. That is why it is so important to translate strategy into an inspiring dream that employees and stakeholders find meaningful.

In the example of Wegmans Food Markets, employees are motivated and inspired by being part of a company with the explicit purpose of increasing the health of its customers. They are motivated by having the opportunity to determine how to use their abilities in ways that best fulfill the company's dream.

Recognition from colleagues and management is another strong motivational factor, as long as it is considered genuine. Empty praise is demotivating, but honest recognition is a driving force that motivates more than money. The feeling of being on the right track and having achieved something with others creates joy at work, even if it is difficult at times.

Most important is the joy of unfolding one's potential and developing with others. Leadership is put to a test here, since it requires a continuous eye for what the individual employee needs to unfold their potential. This is not obtainable with just an annual performance meeting with an employee. It requires constant attention to those involved and an understanding for whether the team is properly equipped for the next season.

On December 1. 1950, George W. Merck gave a speech at the Medical College of Virginia in Richmond. Merck's speech in 1950 did not dwell on the success that had transformed Merck from being a respectable but small pharmaceutical company into the largest in the industry in the United States, which today employs 70,000 globally. Instead, he formulated what we call Merck & Co's dream:

> *"We try to remember that medicine is for the patient. We try never to forget that medicine is for the people. It is not for the profit. The profits follow, and if we have remembered that, they have never failed to appear. The better we have remembered it, the larger they have been."*

For George Merck, profit was not the goal, but a result of a dream of improving or even saving people's lives.

ENGAGEMENT PAYS OFF

George Merck had a strong product, and one could argue that he could easily have let profit come by itself without thinking of people first. But his ideas have since been backed by research showing that companies with a high degree of social responsibility, employee satisfaction and dedication have greater profitability.

Alex Edmans, Professor of Finance at London Business School, has studied the 100 Best Companies To Work For In America, published every year in Fortune. Using data from decades, Alex Edmans has seen that companies at the top of the list deliver, on average, an annual result that is between two to five percent better than their competitors, taking into account factors such as differences in industries and outside events. These companies also more frequently delivered results which surprised the market positively.

A similar study from 2014 by universities in Warwick, UK and Bonn, Germany concludes that companies with engaged employees beat competitors with less engaged employees by 7 to 14 percent in productivity.

It is tempting for us as leaders to believe that it is only a matter of keeping employees happy, especially based on the well-known truth that happy employees are better for the company than unhappy ones. Many companies are therefore very concerned with increasing employee satisfaction. However, this is the wrong focus. Even though there is a positive connection between employee satisfaction and the bottom line, employees' active engagement is a far better indicator for whether the company performs well. This is seen in the results from the Gallup Q12 Meta-Analysis:

> *"With regard to composite business-unit performance, business units in the top half on employee engagement have a 113% higher success rate within their own company, and a 170% higher success rate across business units in all companies studied. In other words, business units high in employee engagement more than double their odds of above-average composite performance within their own companies, and nearly triple their chances for above-average success across business units in all companies."*

Beyond these indicators of success, there are many other reasons why it is advantageous to have highly-engaged employees. It means less employee turnover, fewer absences and accidents, greater customer satisfaction, greater profits and productivity. And yes, greater employee satisfaction.

Gallup explains that dedicated employees are more aware of their colleagues' and company's needs, not their own, because engagement gives them a sense of co-ownership. They make decisions and solve tasks based more on the common good rather than what will benefit themselves in the short term.

It is well documented that employee satisfaction does not necessarily lead to engagement. The Gallup survey 'State of the Global Workplace' shows that while job satisfaction is sky high in Western Europe, where 90 percent or more say they are satisfied with their job, only a small share of employees are actively engaged. Only around 15 percent are described as actively engaged employees who take initiatives and responsibility, while 20 percent are actively non-engaged, negatively engaged to the degree of venting their frustrations and even directly counteracting their colleagues and management.

It seems inconsistent with job satisfaction, and while the two surveys have a different focus, the broad conclusion is that most Western Europeans go to work happy, but fairly unengaged.

Companies with high satisfaction perform better than companies with low satisfaction. However, it is motivation and engagement that makes the big difference in the company's performance and the crucial factor seems to be a strong feeling of purpose and meaning in one's work. If we can't see the meaning in our work, it doesn't matter how good the work conditions are. Healthcare, paid leave and company charities are not enough. It might make some stay longer on the job than they perhaps would because they don't want to give up the benefits, but their engagement will diminish as well as their job satisfaction.

The Dutch consultancy, Corporate Rebels, has specialized in determining what makes companies creative and productive, and what causes employees to go to work happy and engaged. They have visited companies around the world and now consult others in how to create joy through engagement at the workplace. They concluded that companies need to shift focus from profit to purpose; from hierarchy to a network of teams; from management telling employees what to do to leaders asking how they best can support employees; from tight rules to autonomy; from secrecy to transparency.

WE WANT TO HAVE A PURPOSE

Why is it so important to have a purpose? We humans have always had to work – often doing things, we don't really enjoy or feel passionate about. This is nothing new. Henry Ford's workers did not have an aching desire to work on the assembly lines. They did it to earn a wage and support their families. Their paycheck was what drove them, not the job itself or the mission, purpose and goals of the company.

At a time when there were few opportunities to support one's family, that may have been sufficient. But today, it is not enough for most of us to work just for a paycheck; we want to develop and thrive at work. We want to see a purpose in what we do that goes beyond mere economic survival. We want more.

As opposed to earlier times, the digital world we live in has made it all too easy to quickly discover when our job has lost its meaning. Sixty years ago, it was still meaningful to risk one's life digging coal out of the ground in dark, dangerous coalmines, because coal was essential to our collective prosperity. Today however, a quick Google search would tell you that by going down that coal mine, you are putting your life at risk for something a machine could do much better and quicker. Also, you will find that the energy source you are mining is being phased out because it is damaging to the environment and for human health.

The optimal form of motivation is "Grand Will," which, according to Joseph Jaworski, an American leadership expert and author of the book *Synchronicity – The Inner Path of Leadership*, occurs when willpower to complete a job is replaced with willingness. You go to work because you look forward to what you will accomplish and see a purpose in what you do. It is no longer just about oneself; it's about the greater mission towards a dream, which you identify with and which engage you.

Most people want to make a positive difference, and, once again, increased access to information in the digital age plays a big role. You can quickly see if the organization you work for is getting bad press or is having issues with its customers or shareholders. If you come to realize that you are not involved with something positive, but actually work with something that society considers damaging, you easily lose your sense of purpose and engagement.

Alex Edmans' research showed that companies with high employee engagement often surprise the market by outperforming expectations. It is not surprising, however, if you subscribe to Jaworski's idea of what he calls synchronicity. Synchronicity is what he characterizes as strong collaboration and a spirit of unity, which seems to occur by chance, when, in fact, chance has nothing to do with it. Behind it is the shared sense of the grand will: a deeper meaning and greater willingness. This attracts people and can drive them to synchronize their actions and create strong and meaningful collaboration, which makes it possible to perform great feats. An organization that consciously works to create an optimal framework for the grand will to exist has the optimal conditions to perform better.

Grand will works through several psychological mechanisms, including the desire for meaning and to collaborate on achieving a dream. A leadership style that is anchored in a meaningful and relevant dream and that creates conditions so that the dream can be achieved leads to integrated employee motivation and engagement. Traditional performance management seldom, if ever, achieves this.

When the dream, the details and the platform are calibrated and work in harmony, those involved can perform well and grow. The organization's desire to make a positive difference is a part of the dream and its mission and reason for existing. It is not just a CSR policy a department has been assigned to develop and manage. Employees' growth and engagement are not seen as a means to make a profit, but as a goal in itself, because the organization's ability to change seasons depends on it.

BASIC NEEDS MUST BE FULFILLED

Many researchers have studied motivation and engagement. Two are Richard Ryan and Edward Deci, professors at the University of Rochester in the USA. For many years, the two researchers have studied how different types of motivation work on modern humans and what needs must be fulfilled for us to feel engaged and see meaning in our work.

According to Ryan and Deci, there are three psychological factors that are essential for a well-functioning person: our competencies, the presence of autonomy and our feeling of belonging. Their Self-Determination Theory describes the importance of our competencies functioning in the proper context, that there is autonomy to manage and regulate ourselves and belonging to a meaningful team.

Most of us know the feeling of being assigned a task that is either way too easy or way to difficult. In both cases, it can lead to frustration and a lack of purpose. If you repeatedly are assigned tasks that don't challenge your skills, it is easy to feel misunderstood and unappreciated. This feeling can gnaw at you and eventually will affect your self-image, making you doubt your own skills and worth. On the other hand, a task that is well beyond your skillset will just as quickly cause you to be filled with a sense of hopelessness and futility. Both situations exemplify conditions in which the theory of self-determination comes into play.

However, when you are given a task that both challenges you and you have the skills to accomplish, you experience personal growth. Add to this the opportunity to determine what the best solution or path is, and your sense of autonomy – the feeling of having influence on your daily life – is strengthened.

And if at the same time you feel you are placed in the right role in relation to those you work with, your sense of belonging increases; you bring value to the group and contribute to the common goals. Belonging is one of the most important attributes for humans. It is a basic need, hardwired deep in our collective psyche. Indeed, our very survival as individuals and as a species has depended on working together and being a part of a community. Recent research in the concept of robustness points out that robust and resilient systems are rarely dependent on a robust individual, but rather a solid network working together.

When competences, autonomy and belonging are in harmony, we then have a sense of meaning in our lives and can feel wanted and loved. This is the foundation for our self-worth, which is fundamental in our ability to perform at a very high level.

Google uses the term "psychological safety" in the workplace. The term was coined as a result of a five-year study that examined why some teams at Google performed exceptionally well, while others lagged behind. In theory, all the teams had access to the same resources, and Google is recognized year after year as one the world's best and most innovative companies to work for. Google is very diligent about finding the most talented individuals and placed them in teams that should succeed. However, there was a significant difference in groups' performances. A team composed of rock stars was no guarantee of rocking results.

In the study, named Project Aristotle, Google analyzed massive amounts of data to explain the difference in performance, but couldn't find a pattern. Diversity of gender, ethnicity, age, psychological profiles and other attributes were all studied, but nothing definitive came from it. It wasn't until they began working with a team of behavioral psychologists and looked at factors that were more difficult to measure that results began to appear.

They found that the key was in a group's culture. There were five dynamics in particular that led to high-performing teams:

- High dependability – team members could trust each other and trust that things would be done as agreed upon.
- Structure and clarity – the highest performing groups had a clear direction and well-defined roles.

- Meaning – each team member could see meaning in their roles, tasks, plans and goals.
- Making a difference – members felt that their work made a positive contribution to the greater goals.
- Psychological safety – in the highest performing groups, everyone was free to have a say in the work being done without fear of being mocked or ridiculed. They could ask questions or make suggestions without being nervous that their team lead would interpret it as a weakness. There was room for new ideas and to challenge assumptions. Recognition was giving freely, and it was easy to belong in the group. In other words, there was a high degree of trust in the team.

THE KEYBOARD OF MOTIVATION

In psychological research, motivation is not necessarily the same as engagement. Motivation is what drives us and can have several different variations, while, in our experience, engagement is more closely linked to purpose, the drive to be recognized – or actually being loved.

Motivation, in a broad sense, if integrated and meaningful, is stronger than when it is externally controlled. A good salary can make us go to work, but it is the sense of meaning at work that makes us go the extra mile. And when we get to the point where we identify with our role and are inspired by the dream, we can perform amazing feats.

As the philosopher and theologian Martin Buber expressed it, the ultimate state of motivation is the one which *"meaning is so deep that it causes us to feel that we are doing what we were predestined to do."*

In this situation, there is a natural feeling that "this is right," and we work with much greater motivation and self-esteem than the prospect of a mere salary can explain.

This understanding of motivation is an important part of a leader's role, and it also explains why traditional performance management no longer succeeds. Fully-integrated motivation is only created when there is interaction between the dream – the common purpose – and the details, allowing you, in collaboration with others, to develop and perform in a way that is meaningful and relevant to achieve the dream.

People we work with must be placed in a position where they can utilize and develop their abilities optimally, both as individuals and together as a team. The platform for change also plays an important role - it must ensure that there are fewer limitations so that the details can be properly prioritized, and the dream can be translated into meaningful action.

People are driven by a multitude of motivational factors. There is an entire scale of situations and relationships that challenge and develop us. This can be described as the motivation continuum, which we define as the keyboard of motivation. Each of us plays on the entire keyboard, even though we do not use all the keys as often. And while most of us are motivated to do something good for the whole, we are, at the same time, driven by a desire to do something good for ourselves, a desire for recognition, success, wealth, celebrity or to be loved.

The keys on the keyboard of motivation goes from no motivation, with lack of intentionality and personal causation, through extrinsic motivation, with succeeding keys ranging from externally-regulated motivation, containing reinforcements such as gaining rewards or avoiding punishment; introjected motivation driven by a conscious avoidance of external sources of disapproval; identified motivation where personally-held values or learning can be the drivers; to the ultimate motivational factor, integrated meaning-driven motivation, in which our behaviors are fully incorporated into the repertoire of behaviors that satisfy psychological needs.

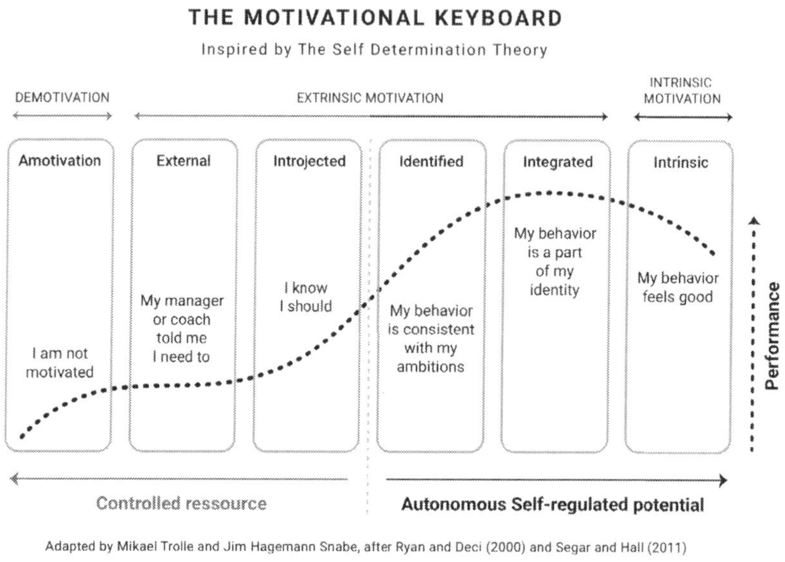

Figure 4: The Motivational Keyboard

The last key on the motivational keyboard is intrinsic motivation, where enjoyment, pleasure and fun is derived from work, and no discernible reinforcement or rewards are needed. Contrary to what many think, the intrinsic motivation key is not the most potent when it comes to engagement – it is more about having fun. In general, the motivational keyboard goes from controlling motives towards autonomous motives, or from low internalization, through high internalization towards a state where it is fully integrated.

People who are motivated only through externally-regulated extrinsic factors, such as punishment and rewards because their job does not allow them otherwise, are at risk of striking the key of demotivation. In the long run, a feeling of demotivation can be followed by a feeling of apathy and depression. People who are in these negative forms of demotivation will have greatly limited desire and performance. They will at first try to cope with the situation, try to endure the meaninglessness, and slowly slip into permanent apathy and with a risk of a physiological depression.

Ryan and Deci consider integrated and identified motivation as the strongest drivers regarding engagement, as these forms of motivation are more related to basic psychological needs. This can be seen as motivation in which you no longer look at your work as a job, but as part of your identity. "Meaning for us" connects to "meaning for me." It creates an extraordinary internal driving force to solve problems and complete tasks.

Traditional performance management, in which the strategic process is locked in a prearranged direction by detailed plans and processes, makes it more difficult to achieve the optimum integrated form of motivation.

This is especially true in a time when reward mechanisms are often built into performance targets that can be overtaken by a changed reality. If there is a conflict between the motivational factor and the reality of the human being, motivation will decrease, as will performance.

In many cases, employees are in the best position to solve a problem, but if it does not fit it into their performance targets, they are faced with being rejected, leading to a further decline in motivation.

ENGAGEMENT IS A LEADER'S RESPONSIBILITY

Some leaders today are upset by the fact that employees are not more engaged and that virtually no initiatives come from lower ranks despite all kinds of wellbeing programs. In many cases, the root cause is linked to a lack of a meaningful direction for the company. At times when market expectations change, this tendency is even more obvious.

It is now, and will be even more so in the future, the responsibility of leaders to ensure that employees are engaged and use their engagement to make themselves and the company more competitive and relevant.

Research and practical experience from our own and other companies confirms that our Dreams and Details leadership model addresses the factors that matter to engagement. The dream can create a fundamental sense of grand will, which translates into extraordinary engagement: "I want to be part of this, even though it will be difficult." Attention to details can help ensure that Ryan and Deci's conditions for competencies, autonomy and belonging have the best opportunities to be met. They fit precisely in the workflow with roles, skills and collaboration, and the development of critical capabilities to achieve the dream.

These psychological factors are the key to understanding why Dreams and Details is a powerful leadership model. A model that, in most industries, accommodates the critical psychological conditions for optimal performance. It is especially needed in a world where digitalization and increased speed requires more motivated and engaged individuals. And it is crucial when companies need to reinvent themselves from a position of strength through frequent season changes.

CHAPTER 5

THE ART OF ASKING THE RIGHT QUESTIONS

"In the long term the most important question for a company is not what you are but what you are becoming."

Dr. Gary P. Hamel, 1951-. CEO Strategos.

"If it ain't broke, don't fix it," goes the saying. But what if that logic is wrong? Perhaps it would be wiser to say: "If it ain't broke, consider fixing it." Most companies that experience success attempt to scale their success even more. With good reason. But if the market or the product you are succeeding in is becoming irrelevant, then it is necessary to consider the alternatives while there's still time.

"While there is still time" is the biggest challenge. The timing of the efforts to fix it is critical and requires that you are able to challenge your own success and assumptions when things are going well. In particular, companies with a long history and strong culture often have a fixed idea of who they are, what they do and how they do it. But what if the elements that made the company successful are becoming irrelevant?

The "What if?" questions are important here. What if a pharmaceutical company's core business in the future is not medicine, but human health? How does this change the dream? What new details does it have to master, and what should the mindset and framework be to enable the transformation? This is not a fictitious example. Pharmaceutical companies are challenged from all sides. Healthcare and private insurance companies no longer want to pay for the newest and most expensive drugs, and the costs of creating even marginal improvements to existing drugs are sky-high. Patents run out and competitors develop versions that are almost identical but sold at a fraction of the cost. It is a 10X change to use Andy Grove's definition of an inflection point, and therefore the pharmaceutical industry is working hard to redefine its role. It is urgent for the pharmaceutical companies to find new ways to stay relevant, and one way could be to keep people healthy rather than sell medicine to patients. The good news is that the market for staying healthy is growing with the size of the population and demographic developments. So, the opportunity is likely to become even bigger than the traditional pharmaceutical market.

A few years ago, it would have been relevant for the leading automotive companies to ask themselves: What if the assumption that electric cars are irrelevant is wrong? What happens when battery technology allows cars to drive more than 500 miles on one charge – or can be charged in less than 30 minutes? What if an electric car is superior to a traditional car because it accelerates faster, has more space and is cheaper to maintain because it has fewer components? Or what if cars become self-driving and can bring people from door to door easily? What does that mean for the business model? Would public transportation still be relevant? Or would a fleet of selfdriving vehicles become the ultimate public transportation system based on individual needs? Would consumers even buy cars?

One reason that Tesla Motors has been successful in creating a new season in the traditional automotive industry is its ability to challenge many of these assumptions. Tesla did not have an ambition to produce the world's best electric car, but an ambition to produce the world's best car. That, combined with the vision to make transportation more sustainable, was the dream that challenged everything we thought we knew about cars and everything we assumed about electric cars.

Assumptions such as electric cars being small, slow and with boring design. Tesla did not want to compete in that category. Tesla was not aiming to be better than the CityEl, a small three-wheeled electric car, but better than Mercedes, Audi and Porsche. That set the bar unquestionably higher in terms of speed, space, safety and design.

Along the way, that meant new ways of thinking about the design of the car. If adding a battery is an afterthought to an existing car design, the battery will most likely take up a lot of space and therefore be minimized. If, however the design of a new electric car takes advantage of the heavy battery to improve the driving experience of the car and increasing the space in the car, the electric car suddenly has a competitive advantage. When you think of the design in this way, you will not try to minimize the size of the battery, but instead make the battery so big, that the car can drive faster and further.

This way of thinking requires that management dares to challenge existing assumptions about who and what the company is, what it can do and what it should do. This pertains to products and customer relationships as well.

In the same way, you should challenge assumptions about what your market is and where it will be in the future. "What if?" becomes the relevant question. Where are the markets of tomorrow, and what league do we want to compete in? How do we become leaders in future growth markets or be a leading team in the best league? There is no big difference between business and sports when it some to questions regarding your future relevance and competitiveness. The crucial question is: What is the biggest wrong assumption we have in our company or on our team in relation to how we think the future will look like and what our role is in that future?

So much of what we take for granted every day may turn out to be wrong in the future. Our assumptions reduce our ability to spot a new season. Part of the resistance to self-driving cars is that we assume that it is too dangerous to let a car drive without human interference. What if that assumption is wrong? Most car accidents happen because of human error. In one or two generations, kids will probably ask us why we took the risk of driving the cars ourselves. "Wasn't that dangerous?" they will ask.

Ten years ago, most of us would probably not have thought that hundreds of thousands of people all over the world would let strangers into their home for the night if they were not home. In 2017 Airbnb had more than 150 million users, 640,000 hosts, and over 100 million projected guest arrivals per year, with an average number of nightly Airbnb stays of 500,000 per night. And the numbers are just increasing.

The assumption of the inviolability of private homes was wrong, and instead, access to private homes became a new market.

Elon Musk, the founder of Tesla Motors, has said that the hardest thing to do is often asking the right questions. As leaders, that is exactly what we need to do in order to challenge assumptions and reinvent our company.

WHAT DON'T WE KNOW WE DON'T KNOW

The former American Secretary of Defense, Donald Rumsfeld, had an important point when he in 2002 spoke about "the unknown unknowns." There are things we know. Then there are things we don't know but know that we don't know. Finally, there are the things we don't know that we don't know – the unknown unknowns. As Rumsfeld said, the latter are often the most difficult. This is also true in business.

So what don't we know that we don't know? And how do we find out? How do we get to a real and open view of a company that is not distorted by everything we think we know?

As a leader, you have a lot of power, to which employees and business partners react. There is a risk that you could be lulled to passiveness in the warm glow of good news, when those around you only say what they think you want to hear. Also, we primarily hear and register what fits into our perception of reality, and we discard more or less the rest, including inconvenient truths. Unconsciously, we construct explanations that fit with how we want to view the world in a form of cognitive dissonance-resolution. For example, we say that declining revenue is often due to temporary challenging market conditions and not due to the fact that our products are getting less relevant due to disruption from somewhere else.

The result is that we don't have the best grounds on which to make important decisions. Unless we can break free of the assumptions and find ways to obtain new knowledge – even the knowledge that we didn't know that we didn't know – we won't improve our ability to understand the future and make the right strategic choices today.

In order to challenge existing assumptions, it is necessary to understand which technologies will have the potential to change the value chain and profitability in the market and thus challenge business models or redefine customer needs. You can initiate the process of challenging assumptions by envisioning the future, assuming all new technologies were leveraged to their full potential. How would it affect the industry? How would it affect the company? Not in terms of science fiction scenarios, but a logical analysis of facts and technological trends. This is often a good way to get a fresh look at the market, a company and its assumptions. Such scenario planning can challenge assumptions and perspectives.

For example, mobile technology has given direct access to consumers. How will it change the opportunity to interact directly with the end-consumer and understand individual preferences? A self-driving car that can be booked via a mobile phone for door-to-door transportation will have a dramatic impact on the assumptions in many industries. How will it change assumptions about transportation and customers' desire to own their own car? How will it affect adjacent industries such as insurance, public transportation and parking services? What new possibilities will be created? How can your company take advantage of these new opportunities?

By envisioning possible scenarios for the future, you can pinpoint assumptions that will be challenged.

Another way to challenge assumptions is to try to envision being a new competitor with endless resources. How would a new competitor look at the market? How would they try to outcompete you? Which technologies would they use and how?

By looking for patterns and trends, and seeing you company from a different angle, you see weaknesses and possibilities that you might have overlooked before. Seeing your company from the outside in based on relevant future scenarios opens a strategic dialogue and allows you to challenge existing assumptions and see new opportunities.

It is also relevant to analyze new players in the industry. In particular, small companies with high growth rates are relevant to study. What assumptions are they challenging? How can they grow so fast? What are they doing that your company is not?

Within science, you often find the most systematic attempts to challenge existing ideas and principles. Scientific methods are inherently made to challenge theories, to examine old truths and attempt to disprove them. People are constantly attempting to disprove even Einstein's theories, regardless of how well known and respected they are.

This systematic approach is very useful for companies to discover that their old assumptions are off the mark or becoming irrelevant and that new assumptions could create new opportunities.

Some of the greatest scientific achievements have occurred through an open, curious and skeptical approach to existing assumptions. Managers have a tendency to react to critical and skeptical employees with negativity, but we have to be careful not to dismiss them. Their skepticism can be very productive.

The first step is to become aware of what assumptions exist in your company. What do we assume about consumers and their needs? What do we assume about the market? What do we assume about our competitors? The investors? What do we assume about the technological and political developments over the next five years?

It often turns out that companies have numerous unspoken assumptions that have become accepted truths. They are often a part of a strong culture and perception within the company, which makes it harder to challenge them and difficult to reinvent the company.

In sports, coaches develop game strategies based on their assumptions of the game. Often, they will not allow the players to challenge them. This limits the development of the game, until someone breaks the assumption. A jump serve in Volleyball was unthinkable years ago, because it was too risky. Today, the jump serve is the norm, because someone decided to practice the jump serve so much, that the risk was reduced. The jump serve changed the game philosophy.

By letting the players dream about how they would be able to play in the future, challenging the game within the framework and inspiring them to play with a new mindset, they will often add new unexpected dimensions to the game and develop the game into new levels of performance.

There are many examples of coaches who limited the game in the first run, but in the long run implemented new dimensions into their game philosophy. These coaches will most likely challenge themselves with the following question; "Why did we not play the game this way in the past?"

This is where the scientific approach is valuable. When assumptions, roughly comparable to scientific theories, are acknowledged, one can begin to challenge them. If an assumption can resist a persistent attack, then it is probably still valid, but it is important to be aware that the work is not necessarily over. Assumptions that are relevant now may become obsolete later.

SEASON CHANGE TAKES COURAGE AND HUMILITY

Hal Gregersen, coauthor of the book *The Innovator's DNA* and head of the MIT Leadership Center, notes that there are common characteristics for leaders who successfully reinvent companies:

- *They seek other people's knowledge and views about themselves and their companies.* They ask customers, employees, business partners, shareholders, and analysts for their opinions. "What would you do, if you were me?" is a question that Walt Bettinger, CEO of the retirement and investment company Charles Schwab, often asks multiple sources to get unexpected approaches and insight, according to Hal Gregersen.
- *They assume that they are wrong.* It is uncomfortable territory for most of us. We are used to having to prove we are right, and traditional management methods with performance targets reinforce this trend. We budget so that we don't end up being wrong. But to change season and to see new markets and opportunities, we have to assume that we are wrong.

When we force ourselves to think critically, it is not to break down our self-esteem, but since a season change alters the rules, we cannot take for granted that we have the right assumptions. To dare to ask ourselves openly where we are mistaken makes it easier for employees to express critical views. It is impossible to learn without making mistakes. The right solution today may be a mistake in the future due to technological developments. Right and wrong are not static.

- *They dare to move outside the corner office's safe and familiar surroundings.* They go out and listen to employees and customers, putting themselves in situations where they are forced to better understand core challenges. They risk exposing their ignorance when they do it but gain new insight that helps when working towards the dream, details and platform.
- *They dare to be silent.* It is not just about listening, but also thinking without making quick decisions on autopilot. It is about giving space to others and listening to their ideas and opinions. According to Hal Gregersen, it is harder for many managers to listen with an open mind without sorting through the filter of

> what we know and picking what fits into our narrative. If we can really listen and ask questions, we will learn a lot. "Ask a question, don't provide the answer," is the mantra.

According to Andy Grove, they are always paranoid about the strength of the company and its role in the future.

This approach does not just help discover a change in season, but also helps identify new opportunities. When we challenge our assumptions about what a company is, and what its market is, then we have a chance to discover new growth markets and imagine our relevance in them. We need to develop our ability to ask the right questions to the right people to get a better understanding on which direction the world is moving and what the company's role should be in the future.

Are outside consultants necessary in this process? There is no doubt that the process of challenging assumptions requires input from the outside. However, we only recommend using consultants for outside-in perspectives and perhaps for help with process and methods. The immersive work of recognizing what your company is, what the emerging markets are and what direction it should go must be done within the company. The effort involves employees and is owned by management.

Such efforts cannot be outsourced. The new discoveries must be felt throughout the entire organization and conveyed with deep conviction. It needs to be an ongoing project for the company because the change of season is not a one-time effort. The ability to reinvent the company from a position of strength becomes the new core skill of companies that want to survive long term – and therefore it needs to be developed internally.

RECOMMENDATIONS FOR CHALLENGING ASSUMPTIONS

- Even though "it ain't broken," ask yourself often: "Are there signs of a new season?" It is better to start when you are successful and from a position of strength.
- Identify the current assumptions within the company, both spoken and unspoken. Challenge the main assumptions with "What if?" and "Why?" questions.
- Consider the potential impact of new technologies on your company's assumptions, value chain, customers and business model. Project an exponential development and assess its impact on current assumptions and business models.
- Search the market for small, new businesses with high growth rates that challenge assumptions in the industry. What are they doing differently? What assumptions do the new players in the industry have? What assumptions have they challenged?
- Listen to customers, employees, business partners and investors – how do they view the company and what assumptions do they have for the future?

CHAPTER 6

CREATE THE DREAM

Change is hard – radical change is even harder. Unless there is a compelling reason for change, most of us try to avoid it – and for good reasons. For most people change means increased uncertainty, unknown tasks, new roles and power shifts. As a consequence, it is generally assumed that radical change can only be implemented if the company has a burning platform. If the alternative is worse, then change is likely to lead to improvement, and as a result, we are more open to change, even if it is hard.

Reinventing an organization from a position of strength is one of the most difficult leadership challenges. In a position of strength, it is normally very difficult to convince people that there is a burning platform and that the alternative is worse. In this case, willingness for change needs to come from something else. What if the alternative is not worse, but much better? What if we could create a burning desire for change?

In order to reinvent an organization from a position of strength, we believe it is necessary to develop an inspiring dream, which can produce the needed burning desire for radical change. The dream should be based on a relevant strategy – but it is much more than a strategy or a financial plan.

A genuine, inspiring dream is not spun out of thin air. It is formed by working diligently with the company's assumptions about itself, its future markets and its strategy, and setting a clear direction with a strong ambition that can rally everyone involved around the role of the company in the future.

A reinvention does not come from simply reorganizing your company, although it may be a necessary step in the process of reinvention. Changing organizational structure does typically not create a burning desire in most people. Reorganizations often cause fear and uncertainty rather than inspiration – in particular if the reason for the reorganization is unclear or appears to be driven by an internal powergames. If a reorganization occurs as a logical consequence of a strategy and the efforts to strengthen the ability to realize the dream, it makes sense and can support the reinvention process. But this requires that the dream is clear and inspires everyone, and that the new structure defines a better framework for the organization to develop the crucial details to reach the dream. The sequence is important.

A company's way of thinking and acting often must change fundamentally if it wants to reinvent itself. This requires thorough preparation. As a leader, you need to ask questions and challenge the assumptions we discussed previously. And you have to conduct a systematic analysis of your company, the value chain and where technology and the market is heading.

The first assumption a company must challenge is what market it is targeting and what role it plays in that market. We can easily overlook the need for a season change if we continue to optimize our current role in the current market to achieve short-term financial results.

The next assumption that needs to be challenged is what differentiates the company, or what is required to be successful in the future market. We have to dare to challenge the assumption that we know what our market is and what our customers want. These assumptions – what the business is and where its market is going and what it takes to win – are central when the first and most important element of the dream, the direction, is defined.

THE DIRECTION

It is crucial for the dream that the company has identified an attractive future market with room for growth and potential for development. At the same time, the market must be relevant for the company. In most cases the essence or the core of the company needs to stay the core. However, if done right, the market analysis will open up new opportunities, where the core may be relevant in a new context.

MATCH THE MARKET WITH THE COMPANY

In order for a company to stay relevant over time, we believe that it needs to constantly look for new growth opportunities. However, a company cannot just pick any new market to break into. A thorough analysis of both the growth markets and core capabilities of the company is needed to find relevant market opportunities. It is easy to find a lot of markets in growth, but the company must also be able to convincingly enter the selected market and make itself relevant within a reasonable period of time. Otherwise the direction will not make sense.

When assessing future growth markets, you will need to give up the sense of control inherent in the process of planning, formulating and diligently following performance goals. As we mentioned earlier, control is an illusion that can block our ability to identify a new season.

You cannot predict the future without risking mistakes, especially when a new season changes the rules of the game. When considering future growth markets, you will have to accept a level of uncertainty and make some risky bets. However, predictions that are based on facts and explicit assumptions, and not pure guesswork or wishful thinking, are more likely to lead to the right conclusions. Where is the growth likely to be? Where are the possibilities for becoming a significant player in the market, not only now, but in five years? What is happening that will change conditions in the market so that it becomes an inflection point?

You should not only examine your current business, but also look at adjacent businesses. For example, one of the biggest challenges for insurance companies may not come from new digital competitors, but from self-driving cars, as they most likely will have very few accidents. Therefore, they are bound to upend the current car insurance market, but will perhaps create opportunities for new ones.

Similarly, developments in technology, including the Internet of Things, 3D printing, nanotechnology, artificial intelligence, circular economics, renewable energy and new service offerings, pose new challenges for existing business models, but also new opportunities.

Do you have competitors that are small but growing fast? Then look at what they are doing. If growth is high, they might be on to something important that you should take seriously. They can point to a market that is developing, even though it looks insignificant in terms of size right now. As we wrote in the previous chapter, it will also help you to imagine how a competitor would challenge your business using new technologies and alternative business models.

Another question you can ask yourself is how you would act if you were a startup with no legacy or old habits. Where would you place your bets? If it's somewhere other than where your business is right now, it may be the beginning of a new season.

WHAT ARE YOUR COMPANY'S STRENGTHS?

According to a study done by McKinsey & Company, companies that are most likely to survive long term are companies operating in growth markets. Profit is naturally also important for survival, but if you have to choose between growth and profit, seeking growth is more important for long term survival.

At SAP, we agreed that the foundation for reinventing the company was to create growth opportunities through innovation. We asked our strategy team to examine the technological developments that were occurring at the time and try to extrapolate what technologies would create growth opportunities in the future. The goal was to determine how future technologies would affect the way companies operate and use that to understand the future market for enterprise software.

The analysis helped us identify a range of potential high-growth markets that were adjacent to the market we were already in. Our job then was to find future markets in which the company's core competencies were relevant, so we had a chance to win.

According to the analysis, there were three technologies in 2010 that had a high probability of impacting our future market:

- **Mobile technology**. Development of mobile technology would become an invaluable tool for allowing companies to integrate remote employees and create new possibilities for connecting companies with customers and assets directly.
- **Database technology**. New technologies in databases were needed to analyze massive amounts of data. Big data would deliver unique insights to most companies, but it required large amounts of data to be sorted and processed quickly.
- **The Cloud**. Lastly, it became increasingly clear that cloud-based solutions, with their speed and simplicity, would be the preferred way to consume software in the future.

Our analysis showed that, as opposed to the Enterprise Resource Planning (ERP) market, each of these new markets would grow rapidly in the following years and be crucial for how companies reinvent their business through technology. In addition, they represented opportunities in which SAP's core competencies and customer base would give SAP a competitive advantage.

There were, of course, other market opportunities with high growth, including platforms for digital interaction such as social media. But these were not relevant for what we did at SAP. It's always possible to identify new growth markets, but if they are too far away from your core, it may not be relevant for your company to pursue them.

Based on the analysis, we set a clear direction for SAP. We wanted to expand the company into three new markets, which would deliver additional value to customers, increase our strategic relevance and create growth. The analysis showed that, within five years, the three new markets would be as large as the entire ERP market was in 2010.

When we redefined our market to include the three new areas, our addressable market doubled. This meant that our market share was also halved, because our market share within the three new markets was close to zero in 2010. So, SAP went from being the market leader in a saturated market to a company with plenty of opportunities for growth.

The direction was clear: we were going to defend our position within the traditional ERP market and at the same time create growth by becoming a leader in the three new markets, all of which had high growth and were relevant to the core of the company.

SAP chose a direction that would double its market size by entering into in three future growth markets, which were new to SAP, but where the company had capabilities that were relevant. The direction was based on a thorough analysis. Three of the important questions that SAP sought answers for were:

- Where are the future markets? Where will the biggest growth be in the coming years?
- Which parts of the value chain offers the highest profitability?
- Where do we have the best chance of becoming the market leader?

There are many elements to be considered in the analysis, but fundamentally, the direction needs to be based on two dimensions related to the market: the horizontal dimension and the vertical dimension.

The horizontal dimension describes the company's potential role in the value chain: How will the value chain develop over time? Where is the growth? Where is the addressable market? Where is the profitability?

The vertical dimension describes the company's potential role towards each customer, or its share of wallet. Where does the customer spend its money in the category? And how much of the total spend is addressable for the company?

THE HORIZONTAL VALUE CHAIN

Analyses of a company's value chain are often based on the current market and rarely on the future. It is often assumed that Kodak, the market leader for decades in the analog photo market, chose not to pursue the digital photo market because it was less profitable. But was that a correct assumption?

It is true that Kodak's value chain in 1995 was entirely based on analog technology. But Kodak could have changed seasons if the company had analyzed the future value chain and the potential in a future digital market – and challenged its own assumptions of what the company's core was.

In 1995, the digital photo market was new and very small. Cameras were inferior and expensive and therefore only attracted a limited number of consumers. In 1995, analog photo technology dominated, with an annual profit pool of almost \$2 billion. Just ten years later, profits in the analog market had shrunk by 80 percent, while the profit-pool in the digital imaging market grew to just under \$4 billion, twice as much as the analog market at its peak.

The most profitable segment of the new digital value chain turned out to be the memory cards. So, if we revisit the idea of challenging a company's own understanding of who it is, Kodak perceived itself as a company whose core capability was to capture an image on analog film, develop the film and produce physical images on paper. It was not wrong; but it was a very narrow definition.

What if Kodak had defined that its core competence was to store pixels of light on a media, so customers could experience the special moment later? This would still be the core of photography, but much broader and future oriented. The inflection point in the photo market changed the medium on which the pixels are stored from analog film to digital memory cards. Had Kodak defined their core more broadly, the company might have had an opportunity to remain relevant and become a leader in the digital photo market which in 2005 proved to be twice as valuable as the analog market was in 1995. In addition, digital technology offered an opportunity to drastically reduce costs of the product and increase quality over time due to Moore's law in the digital world. In fact, it turned out that the digital memory card market was even more profitable than analog film.

This example shows that an entire value chain can collapse, but a new and much larger can rise from its ashes. If you can see this happening in time, you can invest in the new value chain and focus on areas where growth and profitability are highest and where the company's core remains relevant in a new context.

If Kodak had seen the opportunity to repurpose its core in a new context and had projected where the value chain was headed, its management could have realized that the change of season was a huge opportunity. But Kodak clung to the analog value chain, and when it collapsed, so did Kodak.

Understanding the value chain is also important in sports. The value chain in sports can be considered as all the various dimensions of the game, including the serve, movement on the court, the offense and the defense. You can win in the short run by optimizing and using your current players. But if they cannot cover enough of the value chain of competitiveness, you will be defeated in the end. In that case, you must reinvent your game philosophy, develop the potential of your current players or attract new talent. In that way, you can cover more of the value chain of the game to be competitive and win.

THE VERTICAL VALUE CHAIN – "SHARE OF WALLET"

The horizontal value chain analysis tells you something about where the growth and the profits are in the market. When analyzing the vertical market – the share of wallet – you get a picture of how important a supplier you are to customers and how much growth potential there is within the existing customer base.

At SAP, the analysis showed that we had largely won the market for ERP systems. However, the vertical analysis showed that SAP accounted for less than 10 percent of our customers' total IT costs. Most of their IT investments were spent elsewhere. In other words, SAP had an opportunity to increase its revenue from every customer by challenging the other categories of spend in the value chain – like hardware and services.

But the analysis also revealed that the SAP system could potentially lead to a highly complex IT infrastructure, and expensive implementation efforts. These were two cost drivers that could be challenged through a move to the cloud business model.

SAP therefore saw an opportunity to set a direction with new solutions that would make IT solutions both simpler and cheaper for customers, and where SAP would receive a greater proportion of customers' IT expenses.

Like in business the share of wallet in sports defines which elements will have the highest impact on improving competitiveness of the team and winning. It could be the strength of serve, the quality of the defense or the speed of the game. In Formula 1, many teams start optimizing the winning elements for the next season before the current season is over. In sports, we are constantly looking for these elements to compete short term in the current season, and to develop our game philosophy and team for the next seasons. You are constantly looking for ways to maximize the area of competitiveness – horizontally through developing the coverage of the value chain, and vertically through developing the most impactful elements of the game. This way you are leading the team towards playing in the arenas of the future – always moving to a higher competitive level.

Even during a match, it is possible to change your area of competitiveness needed to win. That's what coaches and their staff constantly will try to identify. If you stay with your current area of competitiveness, and it is below what is needed to win, you will be defeated in the end. In sports "reinventing your game" can be done within a few sets, and within a narrow gap of a few minutes or seconds. What can be learned from this is that it is never too late to reinvent your company. The challenge is to be able to do it from a position of strength.

CORE COMPETENCES

Once you have identified new growth markets, you then need to figure out what role you want to play in each market. Analyzing the value chain and share of wallet enables companies to make qualified predictions about what growth markets they best match up with. The analysis will uncover many possible growth markets, but they will not all be equally relevant.

It is important to understand a company's true potential, which, if it challenges its own assumptions, is often far greater than assumed. But it is also important to understand its limitations. The direction must be relevant. Otherwise the dream will be perceived as naive and, as a consequence, will not inspire the needed change readiness.

For example, at SAP we saw that the hardware industry was a big market, but we did not have the skills to go into that market and would not be able to acquire them fast enough to establish a strong position. In addition, the analysis showed that the market had limited profitability.

For some executives, it will initially be both difficult and risky to make decisions about a future market. However, not making decisions about future markets can easily be even riskier.

If you do not dare to reinvent the company from a position of strength, you may soon be forced to do so when someone else opens up the future market and when it is far less likely to succeed. If you wait until you are challenged by a lack of growth or declining profitability, resources for the future markets may not be as available, and your company will be less confident, both internally and externally. On the other hand, there will be less work required to convince stakeholders that a change of season is necessary. This is one of the reasons why many companies fail to change seasons in time and end up restructuring the company based on a burning platform, with lower chances of winning.

A CHANGE OF SEASON – BUT NOT FOR ALL

In many cases, a season change that is identified early will not affect an entire company, at least not in the beginning. This situation usually occurs when the company is still performing well in the current season and its earnings make it possible to invest in the new season. Very few companies will undergo a total transformation all at once.

One of the things Clayton Christensen examines in *The Innovator's Dilemma* is that, even if a company realizes that it has to change season, it still needs to optimize its existing business and bring in revenue. Problems can arise, according to Christensen, because the new season often is disruptive to the existing business. As a consequence, most companies prefer to defend their existing business, instead of disrupting it.

There are several explanations for this. One is that most revenue is generated in the current season. Another reason is that it is difficult to convince stakeholders that there is a need for a season change.

Employees in the current season are usually focused on and incentivized to optimize the existing business and don't always see themselves as part of the new season. At the same time, managers and employees who work wholeheartedly on becoming relevant in the next season are often challenged by the existing business because, at the beginning of the new season, they will appear to be underperforming. Even though the company realizes the need for a season change, incentives and personal motivations may prevent the company from completing the reinvention..

Kodak is one of the best know examples of this. Kodak had invented the world's first digital camera, but its management did not dare to promote the digital technology because it would cannibalize Kodak's entire core business, which was based on film, paper photos and film development in the analog world. So, even though Kodak invented the next season and had the right skills, the company missed an opportunity to become a leader in a future market twice the size of their current market. It is thought-provoking, because it shows that it is not only the identification of a new season that is challenging, but also the execution of the season change, with all the internal barriers, that creates some of the greatest challenges.

Many companies are aware of the dilemma and try to solve it in different ways. One example is Danske Bank's mobile efforts called MobileLife, which was set up as its own company to leverage mobile technology to challenge the existing banking business in a time when new types of banks, branch diversification and deregulation challenged their traditional business model. MobileLife was spun off and kept outside of the existing business to avoid being crushed by of the weight of the classic banking business.

Another example is the Danish company Bang & Olufsen. The company was built on the assumption that well-designed products evolve into classics that customers keep for decades and are willing to pay higher prices for. This assumption is still true, but technological developments have challenged the lifetime of products. New standards for digital TV signals, screen resolution and wireless digital audio have meant that today's customers prefer the latest product that meets the newest technology standards. This challenged the company's business model significantly. The change did not mean that customers did not care about beautiful design, but it necessitated new requirements for the products' technical capabilities as well as the ability to update products more rapidly.

Bang & Olufsen acknowledged that it was necessary to reinvent the company and did so first by investing in cordless portable products tailored to the new ways of consuming media and music. In 2012, the company established a separate brand: B&O Play, which targeted a new audience by focusing on mobile wireless speakers and headphones. High-quality design and sound became the core of the new products.

Bang & Olufsen was able to shake up its original assumption that its products could live for decades in customers' homes. Instead, they managed to accelerate product development and shorten product life cycles, so that they could launch new products and variations every quarter.

In the beginning, B&O Play was the little brother to the traditional Bang & Olufsen and the new brand was challenged by people in the traditional business unit. Today, B&O Play is the largest division and has much higher growth rates and profitability than the traditional Bang & Olufsen business. The process of integrating the new with the old has begun. Traditional products are now also digital and can integrate with the new B&O Play products. Now they just need to use their newfound experience in developing and updating products quickly in their traditional product portfolio.

And even though it's a major season change with new technological and business assumptions, the core of Bang & Olufsen is still the same: creating beautifully designed products that give customers a unique experience, now in a digital world with streaming content, digital user experiences and rapid innovation cycles.

The biggest challenge in shifting from the old season to the new is to ensure that the dream is shared by the entire company, including the parts that work with the existing season. Otherwise the risk of ending up with two competing business units is high. This will be discussed in more detail later in the chapter where we look at anchoring the dream.

RECOMMENDATIONS FOR THE DIRECTION

- Understand the current value chain and project where it is going: Where is the growth within the value chain? Where is the profitability in the future? Which parts of the value chain will be squeezed by new technology or new players?
- Based on the value-chain projection, determine which of future market segments are relevant for your business without moving too far away from your core competencies. Which role should your company play in the future market? By when?
- Analyze your company's share of wallet: How much share of customers' spend in the category does the company have access to? What can you do to increase the share?
- Assess how your company can deliver more value to the customer and increase your share of wallet.
- Based on the analysis of the value chain and the share of wallet, define a clear strategic priorities for the company: which markets will create growth opportunities for the company? Where is the profitability going to come from?

THE AMBITION

For comparison's sake, if we say that the company's direction is the sport it participates in, then its ambition is the league or level it chooses to compete in. Setting the right ambition level is a key element in the reinvention process. It is a question of balance. On the one hand, the ambition can't be unrealistic. It must be relevant and meaningful for it to be possible, especially if you primarily want to base it on internal meaning-driven motivation.

On the other hand, it can only spur change and create a season change if it is ambitious. The entire organization has to feel that things need to be done in a very different ways to fulfill the ambition.

Setting the right ambition requires that you define your addressable market accurately. A small local grocery store in a small village can set a direction of selling locally produced food from organic farmers. However, this direction will be meaningless if the ambition to surpass all other leading national supermarkets. The ambition will appear unrealistic, and then the direction will also be considered doubtful, even though the analysis that this is a future growth market may be real enough.

If you are the only organic shop in the area, it is unambitious to set an ambition of being the city's best organic market. But you can set an ambition to be the region's preferred supplier of organic goods. Or to become the leading organic retail chain with similar markets in other local areas throughout the country. Or having the highest customer satisfaction in the country.

The important thing is to set an ambition to be a significant player in your defined market. The ambition needs to make you sweat a bit when you think how it can be done, but you can still believe that it is possible.

Apple is a good example of this on a global scale. Back in 2001 the market for personal computers was largely dominated by Microsoft, and it was not realistic to surpass them, but Apple instead defined its ambition to be a leader in the market for consumer devices with great user experiences. This ambition became Apple's way of differentiating itself, and it created an almost cult following, which enabled Apple to charge higher prices than its competitors. So, the direction defines the market in which a company operates, and the ambition decides the role it will play in that market.

Or consider Tesla Motors again. With an ambition to make the best cars in the world, all aspects of the vehicle have to be the best – from acceleration and design to safety, handling and the driving experience.

If the ambition had been to create the world's best electric car, Tesla would undoubtedly have looked different today. They would have focused on the customer segment that already bought electric cars, and tried to outcompete the players in just that market. But Tesla aimed to be the best in the Champions League, not just their own division.

Similarly, President Kennedy created a whole new league of technological development when he declared that the United States would send a man to the moon and back again, rather than just shooting to win the Space Race against the USSR. The dream suddenly became much more concrete and much more demanding, becoming the driving force for all the inventions, technologies and innovations that were the product of the ambition to reach the moon.

THE AMBITION MUST BE CREDIBLE

The ambition fuels the dream. To make it real, the ambition has to be relevant, both in economic and human terms.

At SAP, the direction it set doubled its addressable market. As a consequence, it was natural to translate the direction into a financial ambition to double the company's revenue from just over 10 billion euro to 20 billion euro within five years. The new markets represented more than just growth opportunities. If we were successful in winning the new markets, the business model would become relevant for the future, and we could, through scale, increase profitability.

Setting an ambition for increased profitability was also important in order to prevent growth from leading to an increased bureaucracy, which could slow down the company. However, the strategy was not just about achieving a certain revenue or a certain profit margin. To succeed with the reinvention, it was important that we could win in the new markets, not just participate in them. Therefore, we decided that by 2015 we would be the largest or the fastest growing company within each of the three new markets.

The new ambition challenged previous assumptions that SAP could not grow much more. And it sent a clear message in terms speed of change. Doubling in size in five years was very ambitious, but not impossible. The ambition was challenging and an important driver for change. For two of the three new markets, SAP chose to acquire leading companies to accelerate the reinvention process. The acquisitions increased credibility of the ambition both internally and externally.

An ambition's degree of realism is closely linked to its credibility. It must be able to be communicated convincingly – to the company's employees, to customers, to partners and to shareholders. It should cause some eyebrows to be raised, because the ambition is supposed to be noticed. Even if the ambition is challenging, most stakeholders need to believe that it can be done and feel that it is real and not just a marketing tactic. You cannot cheat with your ambition.

In sports, the ambition is always balanced with the team's abilities: what the players are capable of and what they can become. If a coach tries to deceive his players with a false ambition or by making unrealistic plans or goals, he loses credibility. Players will no longer believe that the ambition can be achieved, and motivation and commitment suffer as a consequence. Everything must fit together. It requires analysis, experience, intuition and honesty to be ambitious in the right way.

It is not different in business. The relevance and scope of an ambition is limited by the potential of your company's capabilities. The ambition must align with the dream and consider the capabilities with optimistic realism: How well can we perform in new areas if we maximize the development of the crucial details?

If the ambition seems like a fantasy, or if the leadership team cannot communicate it with transparency, authenticity and personal conviction, it will not move anything. But if the ambition is calibrated correctly it can become a very powerful driving force for change and reinvention.

RECOMMENDATIONS FOR THE AMBITION

- Define the role of your company in the future value chain. Where should the company be on the offensive? Where should it be defensive?
- Define how your company will differentiate itself in the future market.
- Analyze the competencies that your company lacks in order to play the desired role.
- Describe the ambition in a manner that is big enough to drive change and fulfill the dream, but realistic enough to be credible.
- Which level do you want to perform at, and what kind of league do you want to play in?
- Repeat the ambition again and again.

THE INSPIRATION

The former president of the United States, Dwight D. Eisenhower once said, *"Motivation is the art of making people do what you want them to do because they want it."* One of the great conductors of all time, Benjamin Zander, expresses it in a slightly different way, but the essence is the same: *"Success is not about wealth and fame and power. It's about how many shining eyes I have around me."*

People can make great changes when they are driven by determination and enthusiasm. It's not about having fun or doing something that seems easy – on the contrary. Most people have experienced situations in school, at work or volunteer situations which were extremely difficult and demanded copious effort, but where everyone was nevertheless filled with enthusiasm and wanted to solve the challenge because it was meaningful.

Engaged employees are a company's most important resource, particularly in times of radical change. Engagement relies on understanding the meaning behind what you are doing. You must feel that it is important and that you play an important role in making it happen. And you need to be recognized for your contributions and see the achievements.

That is why inspiration is a critical part of the dream. The direction and ambition speak to logic, but inspiration appeals to the heart – the will. It sparks desire and builds enthusiasm and dedication. The direction and the ambition must be formulated in a way that inspires and makes sense for the individual and for all. The direction shows where you are going. The ambition tells you what to do there. The inspiration is the reason why you should do it.

Inspiration is the part of the dream that anchors it in the business and creates a common purpose that is greater than an individual task.

Just like the other aspects of the dream, the inspiration must be genuine, not just a tagline that sounds good but is not connected to reality. If it comes off as manipulative or disingenuous, the thing that should inspire will have the opposite effect, decreasing desire and increasing meaninglessness.

This is what can happen with many traditional corporate social responsibility (CSR) programs run separately from the core business. They often become tacked on to a company's main activities and can easily get lost or be seen like an afterthought.

The inspiration must be based on the purpose of the company. It needs to be an integral part of a company's DNA, intertwined with its purpose. One of the most meaningful things we can do as humans is to make a positive difference in the world. So, it is important that the inspiration speaks to the company as a whole and to the individual's sense of purpose.

THE BOTTOM LINE IS NOT INSPIRATION

Some may say that the purpose of a business is to make money. Of course, businesses must earn money, otherwise they cannot exist, but making money is in most cases insufficient as a purpose to drive high performance and reinvention over a long period of time. More and more companies recognize this and act accordingly.

As mentioned earlier, studies have shown that employees increasingly want a greater purpose associated with their time and labor than just making money. The concept of work is undergoing a transformation, and if businesses do not motivate employees and engage them in a shared dream, they risk having difficulty attracting the skills that the direction and the ambition require. Employees don't want to just go to work. They want to be recognized for making a difference. They want to be part of something meaningful. Something that goes beyond the company itself and defines the role of the organization in society and its impact on progress.

And after all, it is the employees who deliver results, not the shareholders. It is easy for a company to say that they are going to make the world a better place. But to be credible, it must be based on a practical direction and believable ambition.

SAP set a direction to enter three new future growth markets and an ambition to double revenue within 5 years and become the market leader. Why did we not just base our dream on the ambition of doubling revenue? Because it would have put focus on a financial outcome rather than inspiring people to change and reinvent the company. SAP needed to reinvent itself to become an innovative cloud company. This objective would not have been possible to achieve just by focusing everyone on increasing revenue. In fact, a focus on revenue could have postponed the move to the cloud because the cloud business model reduced revenue in the short run. The dream had to inspire people to improve performance in the next season, not optimize the current season.

The ambition to double revenue while increasing profitability was naturally met with considerable enthusiasm from shareholders. Internally, however, enthusiasm was harder to find. Many were worried that SAP would not be able to achieve such an ambitious goal, and most understood that it would require massive changes for it to happen.

This understandably created uncertainty and doubts. The financial goals were not inspiring enough to get employees to accept and drive the needed changes. Instead, we had to translate the financial ambition into something that would engage and inspire the team. We mentioned earlier that a feeling of meaning or purpose is essential to engagement. Engagement and inspiration has to be genuine and an integrated part of the company's dream. If the dream is meaningful and relevant, then the inspiration will be genuine and authentic.

By 2010 SAP had been providing Enterprise Resource Planning (ERP) solutions to companies for 38 years. In other words, SAPs purpose was to help companies manage resources. Traditionally, the resources managed in an SAP system were financials, materials, assets and human resources. But what if SAP could also help companies manage scarce resources such as energy, water or CO2? What if SAP could leverage its considerable base of customers in nearly every industry, from raw materials to retail, to optimize scarce resources, not just for a single company, but across all companies in an entire value chain? What if SAP could help the world manage its scarce resources?

In a world of more than seven billion people and increasing issues due to limited resources, the ability to help companies manage resources more efficiently and the opportunity to make a positive difference in the world was much more inspiring than the company's quarterly earnings could ever be.

Our line of thinking led to the decision to revisit the purpose of the company to: "We make the world run better – and improve people's lives." It was an inspiring dream, one that was about much more than selling software to companies. It would force us to focus on acting responsibly and making a positive contribution to the world.

With this new purpose we realized that SAP had a significant role to play in a world with increasing need to reduce waste. To emphasize the seriousness of the purpose, we decided that SAP needed to be a role model itself. This led, among other things, to an ambitious plan to reduce SAP's CO_2 emissions by 50 percent by 2020 in spite of our ambitious growth plans.

The reinvented purpose was the driving force to spark the internal inspiration needed to reinvent the company from a position of strength. We were not driven by a burning platform, but by a burning desire fueled by a dream of making a difference.

Again, business can learn from the world of sports. Some sports teams will define their dream around victories and titles. However, in the most successful sports teams, you will find that inspiration for the team and the individual comes from improving performance – not just winning the next game.

The simple result – a great bottom line or a 1-0 win – doesn't tell the whole story. Sometimes the result is disappointing, even if the performance has been excellent. Other times the result is encouraging but it doesn't always reflect the performance of the team.

The following incident from moments after a volleyball game coached by Mikael illustrates this point clearly:

"What's wrong, Trolle? We won the game 3-0." The team manager looked puzzled at the thunderstorm that had just passed through the room. I nearly ripped the door off the frame in the locker room. I spoke in all caps, letters as big as the Hollywood-sign. And yes, we had won by a huge margin, as we almost always did at that time. But it was not an acceptable win.

"You just don't get it, man," I said. "It is not about winning 3-0. It is about how we win!"

It was not about winning 3-0, although we of course always wanted to win our matches. In a period of nine years, we had a winning streak of 230 games in a row in the league, winning 17 national titles and qualifying two times for the playoffs in the Champions League. This was quite a remarkable achievement for a team made up of solely Danish players, because there were no financial resources to hire any foreign professional players.

My anger stemmed from the fact that we had not performed well in the game. The performance had been out of line with our strategy and the win could, therefore, not be leveraged for achieving our dream. This was unsatisfactory and a big threat to fulfilling our dream. A threat that was unacceptable, because, if what we called the "Holte-spirit" was lost, we could also risk not achieving the dream. Working on the crucial details to achieve our dream was our focus, regardless of whether or not we won the game.

The philosophy was that "it is not a question of winning. It is the way we perform." There was a clear distinction between the result of matches and the performance in training and matches. Performance was always essential, and the main focus point in order for us to achieve our dream.

So, it is about progress and capabilities that increase the likelihood of winning titles. It is motivation derived from improving the game, which is a greater motivation than the individual results, even in the result-oriented world of sports. Research among many international top coaches confirms this.

It is important to understand that within the results lies a deeper truth, behind which authenticity is found and people are motivated and engaged. We must lead and develop people with a deeper level of understanding in mind. That is what it is all about. It is about performance and reinvention. About fulfilling the ambition, not just about the result.

In business, we often focus on KPIs and outcomes. But these are not inspiring and do not allow debate about why we do what we do or whether what we do is meaningful. Often the strategic intent is lost when we focus too much on KPIs. If the inspiration is going to be genuine and authentic, it requires wholehearted commitment at all levels and dedicated time for discussion about why and how.

Inspiration requires that you translate the direction and the ambition into something meaningful and inspiring. At SAP, the inspiration was to help save scarce resources and thus contribute to a more sustainable world. The dream, "We make the world run better and improve people's lives," brought the strategy to life through a relevant role in society – a role which was grounded in the history of the company and its core capabilities.

SAP's dream of making the world run better and improving people's lives became authentic through our own ambition to cut our CO_2 emissions by 50 percent. It had an important symbolic meaning for us all that SAP itself took concrete actions to reduce resource consumption as a part of the implementation of our inspiration to help others to do the same.

RECOMMENDATIONS FOR THE INSPIRATION

- Assess your company's role in society and the company's purpose. If the purpose is not clear or sufficiently relevant, the company's purpose should be revised and strengthened.
- Translate the direction and ambition into an inspiring story, based on your company's purpose and relevance.
- Get all leaders involved in the inspiration. Make sure you have enough discussion and involvement to keep your inspiration real. All leaders should be able to inspire employees in a convincing and authentic manner.

- Make sure that the inspiration is shared and keep it relevant by involving everyone. Symbolic actions can be of great importance.
- Make sure that employees get the opportunity to achieve personal recognition by being an important and unique part of a shared dream.

A DREAM FOR ALL

Once the strategic direction, the ambition and the inspiration are in place, the company is ready to reinvent itself around a common dream. But if the dream is to fuel a burning desire for change and reinvention it must be anchored throughout the organization. This is only possible when the inspiration is understood and is credible and meaningful for everyone.

This means that the dream should be easy to convey and with as few words as possible. A 40-page description of what the company is and does is not a dream. The story must be so clear and strong that everyone understands it immediately and develops a desire to become part of the dream.

We mentioned earlier an example in which a company reinvented itself by creating new units outside the company to work towards the new season and leaving large parts of the existing business untouched, at least in the initial stages. This can create an atmosphere where the employees who are still in the old season may feel less worthy or excluded from the dream. They may find that people involved with the new dream get all the attention while they themselves are forgotten, even if they deliver most of the revenue and profit for the company.

It is important to ensure that the dream is formulated in such a way that it is relevant for everyone in the organization. The parts of the company focused on optimizing the existing business are as important as the employees experimenting with the new season. In many ways it is the optimization of the existing business that enables the experiments and investments in the new season. It is important that everyone understands and respects this and that management acknowledges it in words and actions. The dream must include everyone, and it must form the basis for a common inspiration.

SPEND TIME ON THE NARRATIVE

It may take a long time and require many attempts to develop the wording that accurately captures the direction and ambition and translates it into inspiration throughout the company. But when that happens, you will know that it's right. And only then should it be communicated, because until then it will not be credible and convincing, and only then can it become the foundation for a burning desire for change.

In all the international volleyball teams Mikael coached, the ultimate dream was to be a respected part of international volleyball and to develop into a team that could compete with the best. We wanted to play with the very best in the sport, and we knew that this dream would be so inspiring that many talented players would be attracted to it.

Many believe that they are already performing at the highest possible level, but with the right dream and dedicated effort, they will be able reach even higher. The dream to play with the best international teams inspired the individual players and the whole Holte Volleyball team to put the needed efforts into training and developing the crucial details. This was the secret to unlocking their potential. If we always played at a higher level of performance in every game, we would open doors to new arenas. Behind each door would be a new challenge at a new level, where we had never been before. Occasionally, we had the opportunity to open the door to an arena with best players and teams in the world. This was truly inspiring for everyone involved.

Even if defining the right dream is challenging, the most difficult step is to make sure that the dream and all its elements are understood by everyone in the organization.

At a big organization like SAP, it required a lot of efforts to make sure that the dream, including the direction, the ambition and the inspiration, is understood throughout the organization and that everyone felt they were part of it. We did this by first involving all senior executives in SAP early in the process. We decided to assemble the top 200 global executives for a leadership seminar at the headquarters in Germany. The seminar started very traditionally with Bill McDermott and I explaining why we thought it was time to reinvent the company. We discussed the market analysis and the signs of a season change. Then we spoke with great enthusiasm about our dream for the company and where the biggest changes were required to reinvent the company. The first day of the leadership seminar ended with a dialogue about the requirements of the next season and the opportunities ahead. We discussed the relevance of the dream and the significance of the changes needed.

The second part of the seminar was less traditional. Instead of discussing the strategy and the financial goals with the group, we had planned that all 200 top executives should test their ability to explain the change of season and the dream in a convincing way. All executives were sent out in groups of 2 to 'coffee-corners' where they had to stand up in front of a small group of employees who they had never met before and explain what they had learned the day before. They were not allowed to use PowerPoint or any other visual aids.

It turned out that it required much more effort and training than we had expected to create the desired enthusiasm from the employees. Fortunately, the Icelandic volcano, Eyjafjallajökull, erupted and delayed air traffic for several days with its ash clouds. This meant that all executives were grounded in Germany for the weekend. This gave us the needed time to practice the story even more – and get it right.

It was a very valuable learning exercise, which helped each leader to improve their ability to explain the strategy in an inspiring way. This type of dialogue with employees in coffee corners was crucial to ensuring that everyone understood the need to reinvent the company – where we were and where we were heading.

The involvement of the 200 top executives was necessary for two reasons. First, we wanted to make sure that all our leaders could present the dream to our employees around the world in a convincing manner. Second, we did not have a detailed plan for how the details would be perfected. Therefore, we needed to involve the entire organization in finding the best path to the dream.

After experiencing how important the coffee corner sessions were, SAP introduced quarterly coffee corner sessions, where all senior executives would engage employees in conversations about where the company was, where it is going, and how it could improve its performance to deliver on the dream. Employees could ask questions and share their views. It was an opportunity to ensure that the dream was kept alive and still made sense – and to ensure that everyone always had the big picture in mind and were focused on the areas where performance needed to improve.

If you can convince yourself and others that the dream is the right one, people will go a long way to be part of the dream and find a way to make it come true. Therefore, it was so important to involve leaders early in the reinvention process and making sure the dream became their own, so that they could convey it in an authentic way to their teams. And because they could see the need for change and the logic behind the dream, they began to take responsibility for making it come true.

Even if a dream is communicated convincingly, there will still be a degree of skepticism in most organizations. Change creates insecurity, especially in organizations that have been through many changes, and employees may be cynical or pessimistic and will want to see the changes before they believe in them.

It is all about inspiring teams to perform at a new level to stay relevant in the next reason. It is about improving performance, not about the results. It is questionable if you need targets or goals at all. In our opinion, targets and outcome-oriented goals can directly contradict the very inspiration that increases motivation and engagement for the individual.

Some believe that the higher you set the goal, the better people will get at reaching the goal. That is unfortunately a common misunderstanding, proved by many sport psychologists. Different circumstances can determine if you win or lose, and therefore, an evaluation of a team and its players must take into account the situation under which the match was played. With the same performance level, great results can be reached against a weak team and poor results against a strong team. So, the exact score in a match does not always reflect the overall performance level. Therefore, it makes sense for the individual and the team to practice performance, and measure improvements in performance rather than only focusing on the results.

Bill Walsh, one of the most well-known coaches in American football said: *"The score takes care of itself."* It's a great way of saying it. Focus on how we act and perform – and the scoreboard takes care of itself.

When we could see that our mindset and efforts to train the relevant details could open the right opportunities, there was no going back. We were motivated by the way we trained, and how practicing the right details increased the understanding of the game, which improved our skills and collaboration. We just had to unleash our potential through training the crucial details that would enable the dream and know that it was within reach. It became almost a calling, driven by a grand will and it inspired every member of the team to develop and unleash their full potential.

RECOMMENDATION FOR THE DREAM

- Spend time formulating the dream so that it can be conveyed succinctly, engagingly, and credibly. The dream must capture the direction, the ambition and the inspiration.
- Consider how the dream and its elements can become anchored throughout your business so everyone understands the big picture.
- Decide how the dream will be communicated to everyone in the organization, so that it is credible, and inspires everyone to participate in making it come true.
- Ensure that everyone in the organization can explain the dream in a convincing way. It takes time and there must be room for discussion. This is vital for the dream to be shared and be motivating.
- Make sure the dream is kept alive by creating an open dialog with all employees, so everyone understands where the company is in terms of reaching the dream and what needs to improve to accelerate reinvention.

CHAPTER 7

THE CRUCIAL DETAILS

In Walter Isaacson's book *Jobs*, he describes Steve Jobs as not only a visionary and forward-thinking leader, but also as very challenging to work with. His leadership style was both visionary and controlling at the same time, and he often switched between two extremes when evaluating employees' work. It was either amazing or useless. And Jobs was always brutally honest about the evaluation.

This book is largely about how leadership can create opportunities for people to pursue bigger dreams and develop people to explore their full potential. Based on Isaacson's description, some will argue that Steve Jobs' relationship with people didn't exactly live up to this ideal. However, Steve Jobs' relentless and uncompromising focus on details, without a doubt, enabled many people and teams to perform at much high levels, even if his management style can be challenged in some respects.

Steve Jobs understood that mastering certain details is critical for achieving an ambitious dream. He realized that to drive radical change, you have to focus on a few details and seek perfection. And he was willing to spend his own time and efforts as a leader to make sure that these details were developed to perfection.

Steve Jobs was aware that the only way Apple could compete was to design products where the user experience was second to non because both the hardware and software came from the same company. One example is Apple's iPod, an mp3 player. In 2001, it was not a given that Apple's iPod would be a success. Apple was not in the mp3 player market. There were several mp3 players in the market in 2001, so Apple would need to have a significantly better user experience to win over existing players.

For Steve Jobs, the user experience wasn't just about the design or the way the iPod worked. It was the overall experience that was crucial: from the actual purchase in an Apple Store to the unpackaging and installation of the product to its daily use, including interactions with iTunes, where the next song was just a click away.

Jobs succeeded. Apple's iPod was a huge hit and became the unquestionably dominant mp3 player. To date, more than 400 million iPods have been sold. The iPod was a precursor for the iPhone, which, with its apps and fusion of devices, has, in just over ten years, reinvented the mobile phone, the internet and the content industry.

In a world where technology advances quickly, Apple's mobile devices have disrupted many companies in different industries, and it was due to Steve Jobs' uncompromising approach to get the right details perfect.

According to Walter Isaacson, many people have paid a high price to work with such an uncompromising, brilliant leader.

The challenge is to develop a leadership style where you can be uncompromising about the crucial details while helping people develop and improve their ability to unleash their full potential on the details that matter the most.

We propose that it can be done. However, it does require that you are both uncompromising on the details and at the same time focused on developing employee performance and potential. Otherwise, you could easily end up becoming the bottleneck.

CHOOSE THE DETAILS CAREFULLY

As a leader, when you are uncompromising about the crucial details, you are in many ways engaging at the micro level. However, as mentioned earlier, it cannot become micro-management, where you take over the employees' role. Instead, it's what we call micro-leadership, focusing on developing employee performance and potential around the crucial details. Spending your time on the crucial details is not about being the expert. It is about demonstrating that the perfection in the relevant details matter – and it is about developing people to seek perfection.

Steve Jobs chose the user experience/design as the pivotal detail that would differentiate Apple from its competitors. Louis Gerstner chose the customer relationship as the pivotal detail for transforming IBM into a service business. In both cases, it was a single detail that became the focal point for the reinvention of the company. In both cases, the leaders dedicated at least one third of their own time to radically changing the critical detail.

Often, as a leader, you are aware of many things that should be improved. When you are embarking on a process to reinvent the company, many areas in the company will be identified that are not performing optimally. Often, leaders implement so-called must-win battles and make a long list of what battles need to be won in order for you to change the business. The problem with a list of 10-20 must-win battles is that you cannot get involved in so many details at once. The ambition level for each detail will be too low, and the change will be marginal in all areas, where instead it should have been radical in the two or three areas that really drive the reinvention towards the dream.

So, the key is to identify the few absolutely crucial details that need radical change and to be perfected in order to achieve the dream. We assert that it requires very active leadership to ensure that the needed radical change succeeds. This cannot be delegated. The other areas of change are less important, and they can be delegated, so that you as a leader can fully focus on what will make the biggest difference.

As a guiding principle, we believe that as a leader, you need to spend at least one third of your time on each of the crucial details in order to ensure the needed radical change. In other words, the most you can focus on in terms of radical change is three details. One or two is often better. As a result, leadership with regards to the details is largely about delegating other areas that might also need to be improved but are not as important in achieving the dream.

This decision is difficult and takes a lot of courage. But it is a vital. It will increase the clarity of the areas where you see the biggest need for change. The better you choose the few crucial details to transform, the more obvious the change will be for all involved. The more time you spend leading the transformation of the crucial details, the greater the changes are likely to be. It is important that the entire company knows what details unlock the potential to reach the dream. By spending your time on them, you lead by example and clearly indicate where and how the reinvention will take place. This focus and transparency will foster meaning, clarity and commitment.

MICRO-LEADERSHIP, NOT MICRO-MANAGEMENT

Like Steve Jobs, we believe that a leader needs to be brutally honest and uncompromising about the crucial details. But it is not about taking over the responsibility for them. It is about developing the capabilities needed in the employees and in the organization so that they can master the crucial details.

This is completely different from managing details in the traditional sense, where management often creates insecurity by controlling the execution, not relying on employees and instead becoming a bottleneck.

However, it's also not just about dealing with the overall strategy and delegating the execution to the organization based on plans and KPIs. To master the transformation of crucial details, leaders must lead the change. We often see this in the world of arts or sports, where instructors and coaches work to unfold human potential and interfere when performance can be lifted and become sublime.

TRAINING THE DETAILS

In sports, it is generally accepted that the dream can only be fulfilled if training of the details is successful. No one can play at the level of the dream if the details and needed roles, skills and collaboration have not been trained.

In sports, we have the greatest success with the development of the details when the players have been included in understanding how the details impact the overall performance in the game.

It's a part of the DNA of many sports teams to constantly create a new season by further developing the existing capabilities for each of the players. As a coach, you think of each player as piece in a puzzle. Each player is selected for the optimal position on the team every year (roles). You can make the piece bigger (enhance skills) or change its color (new skills) by developing the player's abilities within his or her position. Finally, you can make new edges on the piece so it fits better with the other pieces of the puzzle (collaboration). That is how you created a new puzzle – a season change – for the team every year while at the same time transitioning the players from one season to the next. You could describe this as a development program for the players and the team over many seasons based on continuous reinvention.

If you have the opportunity to make an improvement, you should not hesitate. It's important that you are not limited by a detailed plan with pre-arranged actions. The important details need to be put in place for the players and the team at the right time. You should always be looking for improvements or changes that could quickly enhance the performance. Even the smallest details can be crucial to change the game in the next season.

In a team sport like volleyball, players' genetics play an important role. It is difficult to be an elite volleyball player if you don't have the physique for it. The most important part of working with the details in volleyball is to make sure the players are selected and trained for the specific role on the team. Businesses could do well by looking at their recruitment and training in the same way, making sure that the potential needed in the next season is inherent in the employees and ready to be unleased through talent development.

When the details with the greatest impact for achieving the dream are chosen, the next step is to dramatically increase the organization's performance within those details. Micro-leadership thus becomes a matter of developing and unfolding human potential in the crucial details.

After the somewhat unconventional leadership seminar at SAP in 2010, we had 200 top executives around the world who could engage employees in the dream and spark enthusiasm about the need to reinvent the company. What was left was: "How?" How should we change to deliver the dream? What details should we focus on to drive the necessary change?

We decided to focus on two areas that demanded radical transformation to achieve the dream: SAP needed to dramatically increase the speed of innovation, and SAP needed to re-engage with its customers by increasing value and reducing overall IT-costs.

Dramatically increasing the speed of innovation was critical to become relevant for the future cloud business model. In 2009, it took SAP an average of 14.7 months from the start of a software development project until the product was ready to be delivered to the first customers.

This was too slow compared to the new cloud competitors, who were able to deliver software releases on a continuous basis. In other words, it was necessary to fundamentally reinvent the innovation process.

We decided to target a reduction of the average innovation time by 50%. The goal of halving the time-to-market was received with some skepticism internally. SAP was using a traditional software development methodology know as the "Waterfall methodology". The Waterfall methodology separated the innovation process into 3 subsequent phases: Specification, Programming and Testing. Typically, the Specification phase took four to five months, the Programming phase took about six months, and the Test phase took at least four months. With this structure, it seemed almost impossible to cut development time to less than 8-10 months.

We could not cut down on either the Specification or Testing phase without delivering a lower-quality product, which would not jive with the mission-critical nature of our software. Even if we cut down the Programming phase to the bare minimum, we would still not have halved the total development time. In other words, it required a radical transformation of the entire innovation process if we were to halve the time-to-market.

In 2010, smaller software firms were much quicker than SAP. They used newer methodologies to develop software called Agile or Scrum. The Agile method challenged the assumption that requirements of a product had to be specified before programming could begin. Instead, the method prescribed an iterative process with room for learning and creativity along the way.

SAP did not use the Agile methodology because many Agile experts at the time warned against implementing the methodology in organizations with more than 100 software developers. SAP had around 20,000 developers in 2010 spread out in more than 70 offices around the world. In addition, the Agile methodology seemed unstructured and results seemed unpredictable compared to the traditional development methods. In many ways it was the polar opposite of the development method SAP had used to ensure a controlled process with predictable outcomes. Changing from the Waterfall methodology to Agile was a major transformation in the core of the company. At the same time, it was the key to unlock the potential of the company and its innovation power.

We'll get back to the Agile story in the next section, but first, we want to stress why the effort to increase value and reduce our customers' total IT costs also was important in reinventing the company. On average, SAP made up less than 10 percent of customers' total IT expenses. More than 90 percent went to other suppliers who provided hardware and consulted on the SAP system. Our goal was to become a more strategic supplier to our customers by increasing the value and reducing our customers' total IT expenses.

To achieve this, the move to cloud computing was critical. The cloud business model would allow SAP to control all expenses of the customer and work systematically to reduce costs and simplify their infrastructure, while at the same time delivering more innovation and value. Our customers' total IT costs would be reduced, but SAP could increase its share of the spending if we were able to reduce complexity.

The reinvention of the company was largely focused on leading radical change in these two areas – not thirty.

When the right details are selected, they will identify the key areas where an organization needs the biggest transformation. Therefore, the ambition level regarding the crucial details must be high and leadership must be demanding, uncompromising and insistent.

You must challenge existing assumptions and the way things are done. And always be open to learning from others, including other industries that have perfected those details.

RECOMMENDATIONS FOR THE DETAILS

- Choose up to three details that are most crucial for achieving the dream and which require the biggest transformation in the organization.
- Learn from others, ideally in other industries,who have perfected the chosen details.

- Communicate why the details are crucial to achieving the dream and how the organization needs to develop to reach the desired performance level.
- Be specific on the performance level needed in the crucial details.
- Develop a training plan of each of the details and measure progress.
- Spend your time as a leader to understand the needed change within the crucial details. Lead the change and make sure that transformation is closely monitored.

THE ROLES

The first question we as leaders must ask ourselves when the dream is in place and the details are identified is: What roles do we need to master to perfect the crucial details? In a season change, there are often new roles for both business and employees, but it may also be existing roles that need to be transformed or integrated in new ways.

In a season change, existing roles in the organization will often be challenged. When a company like Rio Tinto introduced remote-controlled equipment into the mines of Perth, Australia, the role of traditional miner became redundant. At the same time, new roles became critical in the control centers where remote control takes place.

The role of bank cashier in a bank branch changes when the bank closes physical branches and opens digital customer interaction points. The role of product designer in a company like Bang & Olufsen is challenged when software becomes the critical aspect of product design as software and not hardware defines the main interaction with the user.

In the example of IBM's season change with Lou Gerstner, IBM had an ambition to develop from being a hardware company to a service company. For IBM to realize the dream, it was necessary to take on a role as strategic advisor for customers, providing them an opportunity to develop the customers' overall IT setup.

The shift in IBM's relationship to the customer also meant a significant shift in the roles within the company. Previously, IBM's success depended on having capable hardware salespeople. But now it was necessary to develop new roles advising customers on how to improve their business by leveraging IT.

IBM tried to develop new roles by setting up a separate consulting entity, IBM Consulting Group, and recruiting experienced consultants from the market to the new entity. However, after a few years, IBM had to acknowledge that it was too slow to develop the new role as strategic consultant organically. Instead, IBM purchased PwC Consulting with 30,000 management consultants for $3.5 billion. This way, IBM could play the role it had chosen, and this new role became central to the transformation of company.

Many companies now realize that software and digital skills are crucial to achieving their dream in the next season. Yet, it is not enough to hire software engineers and set up a separate software unit. If the company wants to enhance physical products with digital capabilities, the new digital skills need to become an integrated part of the processes within the company – from strategy to business model development, product design, sales, support and service delivery.

Tesla Motors is a good example of this. While Tesla in many ways designs traditional cars, their designs are influenced by software. It's one of the ways that Tesla differentiates itself from other car manufacturers. Traditionally, it has been necessary to buy a new car to gain access to new features like dynamic distance control or automated parking. But in a Tesla, you can just install new software, which will enhance the existing car. This can only be done because the roles related to software and upgrades are integrated into the design of the physical car. The car designers at Tesla must be proficient in software and include the unique capabilities of software into the car as they design it.

At SAP, reducing product development times in half required a radical transformation of the development process, and the introduction of Agile meant that the previously vital role of defining detailed product specifications became redundant. Instead, two new roles were crucial to mastering the details of the new development process: the Product Owner and the Scrum Master. The Product Owner is responsible for prioritizing product requirements and defining the minimum scope for the product. The Product Owner ensures that the team works on the right things. The Scrum Master is responsible for keeping the team working efficiently and aligned with the customer and helps ensure that the team is successful. In other words, the Scrum Master makes sure that the team is working in the right way.

Both roles were new to the organization, so we needed to train people in the new roles and we needed to decide how to integrate the new roles into the processes of the company. In order to train the new roles, we decided to test the new development method. We selected three critical development projects as pilot projects. The criteria for the pilot projects was that the projects needed to be large enough to prove that it would be possible to use Agile on a large scale. They also needed to be important enough that so that skeptics would be won over if they succeeded.

In all three pilot projects, the Agile method proved to be significantly better than the traditional waterfall method. The innovation process ran faster, and the products were much more aligned to customer needs. In addition, the employees were excited about the new methodology because they could spend much more time on innovation and dialogue with customers than before – and less time on bureaucracy.

Based on the positive results from the pilot phase and experience with the new roles, the Agile method was rolled out in the entire development organization over a period of three years. It was a very ambitious project, which was only possible due to optimization and fine-tuning that occurred during the pilot projects and the hard work of a transformation team mastering and coaching people on the new methodology and their new roles. The development of the new roles was critical to succeed with the reinvention of the company.

This example from SAP shows that developing and integrating the new roles into the key processes of the organization opens up new opportunities. For a digital transformation to happen, software, technology and data enable a collection of important knowledge of the market and the customers. The right roles integrated in the right way can create new products and services and enhance business models to disrupt competition and create a new season in even very mature markets, just like the case of Tesla Motors.

LEADERS ASSIGN ROLES

In the world of arts, the actor, the violinist and the ballet dancer know how his or her role shapes the overall outcome. On team sports, each player knows what their role is and how it fits into the strategy of the game, so that the dream can be achieved.

In business, the division of roles is not always clear, and in a season change, great uncertainty and frustration can arise when the company rearranges roles. In these situations, existing roles must be reinvented so that the new capabilities are integrated into existing roles. At the same time, some of the existing roles may become redundant. In some cases, completely new roles must be introduced to ensure that the organization is able to capture the new opportunities – organically or through acquisition.

For example, the development of Apple's language processing capability, Siri, required new roles in the company like speech recognition experts and data scientists within the field of artificial intelligence. In order to ensure the new roles were developed fast enough, Apple decided to acquire them. Siri was a spin-off from a project originally developed by the SRI International Artificial Intelligence Center. Its speech recognition engine was provided by Nuance Communications. Siri also needed advanced machine learning technologies to function. These were all roles that did not exist within the company at a high enough level. Because speech recognition was seen as a strategic capability, Apple had to master it to perfection in-house.

When a critical detail requires a new role in the organization, micro-leadership may be needed to ensure that the new role gets the necessary attention, development and protection. The pilot projects at SAP were implemented with a lot of management attention. We knew that the outcome of the pilot projects would be decisive for our ability to roll out the new roles in the entire organization. Often, such a change will create resistance among existing roles when their influence is reduced. The leadership team must ensure that everyone understands why the changes have been made and why the new roles are necessary if the company is to realize its dream.

People have an amazing ability to adapt and develop, as long it provides meaning to the individual. The dream creates meaning and the development of the new roles produces motivation and development opportunities. When leaders make it clear how the role fits into the big picture and supports the transformation towards the dream, the change of roles becomes meaningful and inspiring.

THE ROLE IS AN IDENTITY

While an actor can assume a role that is completely different from their true identity, it is somewhat different in business and in the world of sports as well. Here, a role forms an identity that becomes part of the employee's self-image. It becomes an important part of how the employee is seen by others, both inside the organization and externally with customers, the media and other stakeholders.

As mentioned earlier, people are driven by the need for recognition, and this is where the narrative of the new role is particularly important. The role must provide opportunity for recognition by others when it is done well. How one is perceived within an organization is important.

In the sports world, you may, for strategic reasons, decide to put a player in a position that has a greater risk of making mistakes and looking bad in the eyes of the crowd and the media. This can potentially have a negative effect on the player's self-esteem if he or she does not understand that taking chances and risks will increase the likelihood of success for the team. In this case, the leader must make it clear to the team and others, why he or she is taking a calculated risk and publicly recognize the player for playing to the best of his abilities in a difficult situation. When everyone understands their roles and how they form part of the whole, and at the same time is respected for it, they can make the most of their skills and grow as individuals and as a team.

If the narrative behind the role is not transparent and clear, if the players cannot see how they fit into the bigger picture and if the coach and team do not provide adequate recognition, the players will either lose self-esteem or focus on their personal objectives. They may begin to play their own game to get recognition from the audience and praise from the media instead of playing for the team's benefit. We know this from sports where a team with arguably the best players in the world can lose to an average team, because the average team played as a team and not just as a group of world-class individuals with individual needs and perspectives.

The same mechanisms can be seen in business. If employees cannot see what their role plays in the bigger scheme of things, or if the role does not provide adequate room for recognition, as a psychological need, as we outlined in chapter four, the engagement of the employees may dissipate, and the organization will not perform to full potential.

As a leader, you must clearly communicate which new roles are critical to build the capabilities needed to reach the dream. To make room for the new roles, changes and reductions to the existing roles are needed. Employees need to know how they fit their roles and how their roles fit into the bigger picture. This also applies to departments and teams. They also have a role that they must be able to identify with, and which they feel is crucial to deliver on the dream.

RECOMMENDATIONS FOR THE ROLE

- Identify the roles in the company that are crucial for developing the crucial details, and what roles are redundant or lose significance to a substantial degree.
- Make sure that the new roles are clear and fully understood by employees, but also accepted by the organization. They need to understand the big picture and how the roles lead to fulfilling the dream.
- Decide how to best develop the new roles. Are there existing roles that can be adapted? Are there new roles that need to be acquired?
- Make sure that the new roles are developed at the highest possible speed. Evaluate the progress relative to the difficulty of the task.
- In-source new critical roles and make room for the new roles to grow. It is often necessary to reduce existing roles to provide room, adequate attention and influence for the new roles.
- Be prepared to change or break up existing power structures in your company. It is often necessary to change governance and meeting structures to ensure that the new roles have the needed influence in the organization.
- Create visible positive examples where the new roles play an important role. The organization needs to see the benefits of the new roles and how to act in the new roles to be successful.

THE SKILLS

Skills are closely linked to the ambition and how a company chooses to differentiate itself in the market. A company's differentiation determines which skills are needed to fulfill its ambition and implement a change of season.

At Apple, the crucial detail for reaching the dream was as mentioned earlier user experience. This meant that skills such as industrial design, software design and usability were crucial. The Apple team that developed the first iPod was designing a product that could store "10,000 songs in your pocket," as the slogan went, and have a long battery life.

To deliver on the promise, the skills around hardware needed to be further expanded, otherwise the device would become too big. At the same time, Apple was faced with the need to master new skills that had not been needed previously. They needed to manage music content in a user-friendly and intuitive way that also complied with copyrights and other laws. This included the ability to negotiate with record companies. In this context, significant new skills were needed to manage digital rights so that record companies were not at risk of having their property copied.

Until Apple launched the iPod, users were forced to rip content from CDs or participate in illegal file sharing via Napster, Kazaa and similar services to get content for their mp3 players. Record companies were interested in cooperating with Apple because they developed skills to manage digital rights so that it was easy for users and less risky for record companies. The dream of the iPod with 10.000 songs connected to iTunes with millions of songs sold at 99 cents was so radical that it completely transformed the entire music industry. But if Apple had not developed the new skills, the iPod would have been like all other mp3 players. It was absolutely essential that Apple was focused on these few, but vital skills, and developed them faster than their competitors.

As with the example of the iPod hardware, there are sometimes existing skills and capabilities that need to be taken to a new level. Some skills are new to a company and need to be developed from scratch – or acquired from the outside.

At SAP, the critical detail for achieving the dream was developing software twice as fast. We assessed that the company could develop the skills themselves. However, it required extensive training and radical changes to increase performance so dramatically. Existing assumptions and habits had to be challenged. It required learning from smaller, faster companies, and it required a major commitment from senior executives to support the change. We spent a lot of time studying Agile development methods so that we could challenge wrong assumptions and lead the change of the development process.

But of course, speed was not the only requirement to reinvent the company. Our products also needed to be appealing to customers. Software developers therefore needed to better understand customer needs. In order to improve the ability to design appealing solutions, product managers and developers were trained in a new method, Design Thinking. This method ensures that development teams understand customer needs and build creative solutions that are both technically feasible, economically viable and, above all, desirable for their users.

The cloud business model made it necessary to simplify the software for the customer. In spite of substantial progress in the innovation process and new possibilities for designing desirable solutions, it became clear that the company was unable to develop all these new abilities organically. In particular, the ambition of becoming a leader in cloud computing was a major challenge within the ambitious time-frame. In addition, the business model was challenging because revenue would be very low in the first years, no matter how fast the innovation process. In addition, the company did not have the necessary experience in developing and delivering cloud solutions.

We acknowledged that there was a need for new skills and abilities that we could not develop quickly from within. Therefore, we decided to acquire leading cloud companies in the market to accelerate our transformation. From 2010 to 2013, we spent more than $12 billion on acquisitions. The transactions gave us a quantum leap forward and access to world-class cloud capabilities. Instead of integrating the acquired cloud companies, we decided to transfer our own cloud activities to them and accelerate their speed. The acquired companies all utilized the Agile development methodology and could therefore also help accelerate our transformation of the innovation process.

As the example from SAP illustrates, it is frequently not sufficient to expand existing skills during a season change. Often new skills are needed. At the same time, there may be capabilities that have so far been important in the company but may lose some or all of their significance in the new season. An important leadership responsibility is to assess whether an organization can develop new skills quickly enough internally, or if it needs to acquire external skills.

SAP chose to acquire relatively large cloud companies that were leaders in their niche markets, so that they would be strong enough to continue to develop their skills within SAP. A small cloud company would risk being overrun by a large company like SAP and would not be a catalyst for increasing cloud capabilities.

As digital technologies change products, customer relationships and business models, most companies need to develop new digital capabilities. The ability to combine physical products with software and digital platforms can be crucial to a company's performance in the next season.

Many companies have traditionally outsourced software development and information technology, which made sense in a season where software was only focused on supporting efficiency and was not vital to their strategy. However, if software becomes strategically important for the future of the company, the decision to outsource the function must be challenged. Instead, management should consider insourcing the critical skills in the technologies that shape the next season.

Tesla's dream of building the world's best car demanded that the company be able to differentiate its cars in a way that would give it a competitive advantage in the future car market, in addition to the usual standards and expectations for vehicles.

Tesla decided to differentiate their cars in a number of areas. The cars would be 100 percent electric; it would be able to be enhanced through software updates and it would become self-driving.

If the car was going to stand out on those points, they needed special skills at Tesla, which at the time were not possessed by their competitors. The skill to develop batteries and power management software was critical. The skill to manage software upgrade cycles was critical, as was the skill to develop internet-based sensor systems and sensor data through artificial intelligence.

Tesla realized early on that these skills would help the company differentiate against traditional car manufacturers. The dream of reinventing transportation enabled Tesla to attract the best engineers in these areas and develop the skills long before competitors discovered that they were necessary in the next season. This is one reason why Tesla was able to reach a higher market value than General Motors, despite the fact that Tesla only produces a fraction of the more than 9 million cars per year produced at General Motors.

LEARN FROM THE BEST

When you have identified the skills that are crucial to differentiate your company, it can pay off to learn from other organizations who best utilize those skills. Often you will find them in other industries.

At SAP, one of the biggest levers to accelerate our transformation was to accept that we were not the best at everything, even though we felt that we were market leaders. As a market leader, you easily assume that there are not many companies you can learn from. Learning from number two in the market does not make much sense.

However, the goal of a halving our development time and dramatically improving the usability of our products was so challenging that it forced us to seek knowledge from companies in other industries. We decided to create a "Winners Quest" in which SAP leaders would visit other companies that had world-class skills we needed to learn.

Among others, we visited EA Games - one of the leading virtual gaming companies. They are known to have a good understanding of their end-users and receive feedback from several million users to improve their games. At EA Games, we learned a new rule that challenged some of our assumptions. EA Games has a rule that they would never release a game if the game did not create visible joy in less than 7 minutes. They knew that games that were too complicated to use would never be successful - and therefore they introduced the rule of visible joy in 7 minutes. We took the new rule home in SAP's development department and challenged our assumptions about simplicity of use in business software.

We also visited other companies to learn how to speed up the innovation process. We learned, among other things, LEAN principles from Porsche, and we learned Agile development methods from the smaller, but faster software companies in the industry. One valuable lesson came from Cisco, where we learned how to accelerate the innovation process through acquisitions by not swamping the acquired company with bureaucracy and limitations. This lesson was crucial to the acquisitions we later made. We allowed the acquired companies to grow and succeed outside of the large SAP organization instead of integrating them as we normally would have done.

The greatest lesson was that, even if you are a market leader, you must always be humble enough to challenge your assumptions and learn from others – in particular when you want to reinvent the company.

IS EVERYONE NEEDED?

In a season change, some parts of the business become less relevant, while other parts of the business become strategic. If certain parts of your company are based on skills that are no longer necessary, you must quickly assess whether it is realistic for existing employees to develop the new skills or whether the team needs to be changed more fundamentally.

To realize the dream, you often must be willing to reduce resources within areas that will not be essential in the future. This creates room for new skills and shifts focus from the old season to the new season. Without the reduction, you may not be able to pursue the new opportunities.

This shift will naturally cause some insecurity among employees, who may fear for their future in the company. But our experience has shown that not shifting the skills to the future growth markets will in fact have a bigger negative impact on existing jobs in the organization.

We should not fall in the trap of protecting old irrelevant jobs. Instead we should dedicate our leadership to developing the right skills and give people opportunities that are future oriented. If we, as leaders, create a dream that is strong and inspiring enough, many will want to play a part and contribute where they can, even if it requires radical changes.

When we lead the reinvention of SAP, it was, first and foremost, the middle managers who found it difficult to see themselves in their new roles because the roles and the power base had changed so significantly. This will be discussed in more detail in the next chapter about the platform for change, but the point here is that almost all employees had skills that could be fine-tuned and developed to be relevant in the new season.

Leaders must decide which skills should be developed first. The company cannot do it all at once, so it is necessary to prioritize and sequence the efforts in the right way. The ability to reduce resources in areas with less strategic relevance is the key to unlocking opportunities for the company and its employees to develop relevant skills. Shifting skills and jobs from the old season to the new season is critical to the success of the reinvention efforts. How management handles this shift is important. In most cases existing employees can be developed, and therefore should be developed. However, it is likely that some employees will become redundant. Such situations must be handled with clarity and speed and with a high degree of responsibility and respect for each individual. This is key to ensure the needed credibility and trust internally and externally, and can help accelerate the reinvention efforts, if done right.

RECOMMENDATIONS FOR SKILLS

- Define what new skills your company should have to develop the crucial details. The skills should align with how you differentiate your company to achieve the dream.
- Define which skills need to be in-sourced, which can be outsourced and which skills are no longer needed.
- What new skills can your company develop? How do you acquire and develop the crucial skills fast enough?
- What skills are needed first? Not everything can happen at once, and the correct sequencing is important.
- Spend time and resources in training the crucial skills.
- Learn from companies from other industries that are best at the desired skills.
- Revisit the role of management and reduce the number of hierarchical levels if possible.

- Handle possible redundancies with speed, clarity and respect. If possible give people a chance of a future elsewhere.

THE COLLABORATION

In order to develop the crucial details, we have described the need to define the roles that individual employees or groups need to have and the skills that should be developed in the roles in order to perform optimally in the critical details. The last dimension of developing the details is collaboration. Collaboration is the relationship between roles. It boils down to this: which roles should work together in what way to create the best conditions for achieving the dream?

Similar to sports and the arts, collaboration requires an understanding of the roles others play and their interdependence. Collaboration must be meaningful on four levels. It should make sense for the individual, for the team, for how the team interacts with other teams or departments and for the overall game plan to fulfill the dream.

We have all experienced a game in sports where the people play so well together that you think they are reading each other minds. It's almost like watching a choreographed dance. Even though nothing is planned in advance, the collaboration has been practiced over and over again. Despite the unpredictability of the game, every player is exactly in the right place at the right time. They simply understand the game in a way that allows them to predict what will happen and can move to the right place at the right time.

The same can be achieved in a company. That's what can happen when everyone understands how their role fits in the dream, recognizes the roles of others and knows the limits of their abilities. When everyone works towards the same dream and can see how to get there by using their abilities in collaboration with others, something almost magical can occur.

COLLABORATION MUST BE PRACTICED

For such magic to occur, leaders have to enable employees to work freely and to collaborate without instructions. In the world of sports, the coach trains the team in the roles, the skills and the collaboration that allows the team to bring it to life in a match. Imagine an opposite scenario in which the coach had planned in advance exactly what each player would do during the match, every play and pass, and how many points each player would score. This would make absolutely no sense. It also makes less and less sense to operate this way in business, because circumstances are changing so rapidly and unpredictably – in particular when an industry goes through a season change. Teams and companies perform much better when everyone understands the overall "game philosophy" and when the right roles and skills are in place and can work in sync without interference.

Collaboration is about how roles relate to each other. It is about understanding the relationship between the game and the actions. To understand this interaction, everyone involved must try to get on the same page and know what they have to do to perform.

In team sports, we see collaboration as a series of actions in sequence, consisting of, for example, touches on the ball by individual players. When the game works optimally, it has a rhythm, almost musical, where elements appear naturally and in balance with each other. To fully understand this, we have to dig deeper down into the interdependence of the individual elements. This understanding is essential because only looking at the individual ball touches doesn't take into account what happened leading up to the ball touch. Each ball touch has its own narrative or story, just as each situation in business can't only be measured by a number, but has to be evaluated in the bigger context.

If you understand the interactions, you understand the game. This is the starting point for the ability to interact in the game, enabling you to predict and read the game intuitively. To play a reactive game is not enough to win. The game is too fast for you to merely react. You have to anticipate the game and be proactive. It is tempting to compare it with the conditions of digitization, where existing collaboration may be too defensive and too slow to base your future digital competitive strategy on.

Each employee needs to understand how to collaborate, both as a team and individuals, to achieve the dream. This takes practice and it requires clear communication so that everyone can see how their role fits with others.

Transparency is absolutely crucial. In sports, you can hold tactical meetings with the team prior to a match to cover: who does what, what tactics to use, what the ambition is, what to pay special attention to, who covers the opponent's best attacker, etc. After the match you evaluate the game by going over what went well, what needs work, how to improve before the next match and so on.

At SAP, when we introduced the Agile development processes, collaboration in the product development organization was redefined. Previously, different parts of the organization had been responsible for separate phases of the innovation process. The specifications of a new product were prepared by one team and handed over to another team responsible for programming the software according to the specifications. And finally, a quality assurance team would take over and test the software according to the specifications. With the introduction of Agile, the roles for writing specifications, developing software and assuring quality were combined into self-organizing teams responsible for all roles. Earlier, there was a clear division between the roles. This is exactly the same as in team in sports, where the players are working on their roles, skills and collaboration during practice, preparing to play the game themselves, with their coach as the leader on the sideline, not intervening during the matches.

Each Agile/Scrum team at SAP had all the necessary roles and skills to define and deliver a finished product. Instead of transferring a semifinished product to another team, the Scrum team was responsible for the entire product life-cycle and also for the success of the product.

The different roles in the Scrum teams work very closely together and meet every morning to review the progress and challenge each other. Through close collaboration in the team and frequent dialogue and collaboration with customers, productivity and creativity increases dramatically. This is very similar to briefings, scouting reports, tactical meetings and debriefings in sports.

The Agile methodology introduced a new way of collaborating, which created space for new ideas to be exchanged during the process. It encouraged self-organizing teams to interact, experiment, prioritize and learn at high speed. And it empowered the teams to find the best solutions and perform at a new level.

The new way of collaborating in the development department enabled a dramatic improvement in productivity and a significant reduction in the time to market. In addition, the frequent collaboration with customers ensured increased product relevance and value.

In many ways, the Scrum cycles in Agile development, with frequent customer interactions, was like getting input in the middle of a match. Getting new feedback from customers helped the team understand what was going well and what needed to be improved. It allowed for continuous improvement of performance and at the same time opened the door for recognition.

BE HONEST ABOUT PERFORMANCE

Recognition is important for motivation. The question is what to base the recognition on. A group of employees may have performed heroically and still end up with a weak result. For example, the market might nosedive unexpectedly, or a project was just too risky. And conversely, a team might achieve an excellent result without really having performed at all. Don't confuse good market conditions with good performance or good leadership.

Working in international volleyball in the early 1990s, we developed "VolleyAnalyzer," a software program that was one of the first in the market that could identify the relationship and interdependence between data in a sequence of actions in a volleyball match. The software was inspired by a group of Americans who had worked with game data for some time. We could analyze all connections between elements of the game in our own or the opponent's first wave of attack. This gave a new and deeper understanding of the game, and many games today are won because of such insight into the game. The trick was to assess the real value of numbers and not blindly trust the data. But the data taught us something about the game and also about what was going on, especially in between the numbers.

We recognized that the game was more than numerical values. Each value should be judged in relation to a deeper narrative of the game, especially with respect to the player who had a personal perception of the circumstances behind the individual numerical value. If that understanding was not part of the assessment, then the numbers were meaningless for the players, and they would play the games only with the statistics in mind. This is exactly as if an employee goes after a target goal without considering if it contributes meaningfully to performance.

If the numbers are used in the wrong way, motivation and performance will not improve. On one of our men's national teams, we had a talented player called Anders. In a national match, he performed poorly. After the game, the data confirmed that Anders was attacking at a low level in the game. At the match debriefing in the locker room we reviewed the facts, and Anders was challenged in front of the whole team.

"Anders, damn it, we can't win the game when your attack efficiency is so low." This was a classic mistake when assessing a result based on the numbers. Anders looked up, not saying anything, but he was probably thinking: "You know coach, I am also unhappy about it. But did you really see the match? I was attacking against a huge block matchup from our opponent during the whole match. Not an excuse, but that gave room for all our other attackers. If you think I really did have a problem, why didn't you help me improve instead? I only heard complaints during the time-outs. Why didn't you tell me what to do to improve? And as my coaches, could you let me know when you have created a training regime for me to help me develop in that area? We can't change the numbers now, but maybe we could have if you have coached me differently."

The incident clearly demonstrates that it doesn't make any sense to beat people up over their results. Instead, you have to consider the following: 1) Did you help them along the way? 2) Do you understand the underlying performance, the numbers and the story behind it? And, 3) Do you know how to use the results to help your team perform better in the future? The numbers alone are useless.

Engagement hinges on an individual's role, their development, the feedback they receive and how it balances with the challenges they face to reach the required performance level.

The entire team must understand how to collaborate and define their roles with great transparency. Otherwise it doesn't work. How can you ask a team to play together if they have different perceptions of what they are supposed to do?

A team that understands the game can see each other's competencies blossom during the game and will play optimally under the given framework. Each player will move freely according to an agreed upon mindset, and has a clear understanding of what everyone's role is in reaching the dream. Each becomes a visible and meaningful part of the shared dream.

It is performance that must be at the center of recognition, not just the result. A good result is not an excuse for poor performance, but by focusing on improving performance the results will probably follow. Not every time, but the likelihood for good results will increase.

Honesty is just as important as recognition. To perform optimally, an organization should not only recognize areas with best progress. Progress comes from identifying areas where performance can improve. It is particularly important to create a culture that seeks improvement. It's about being brutally honest and constantly challenging the existing way of working, while at the same time recognizing great performance – not just great results.

RECOMMENDATIONS ON COLLABORATION

- Define which roles and skills should be in close collaboration to develop the crucial details to perfection.
- Train and optimize collaboration in the most critical areas.
- Revisit the leadership structures and eliminate unnecessary bureaucracy and processes that hinder the right kind of collaboration.
- Create incentives around improving performance – not results. Measure the critical collaboration – not individual efforts. The incentives should motivate the right kind of collaboration.
- Celebrate desired collaboration to make sure everyone knows what good looks like. Be brutally honest and transparent about the areas to improve.

A CULTURE OF PERFORMANCE

One of sport's most legendary leaders is NFL coach Bill Walsh, who coached the San Francisco 49ers for a good deal of his professional life and led the team to an extraordinary number of victories. His book, *The Score Takes Care of Itself*, is about American football, but it is first and foremost his leadership philosophy, based on a deep understanding of human psychology and motivation.

The book's title, *The Score Takes Care of Itself*, refers to Walsh's conviction that if you practice the relevant details long enough and focus on delivering the best possible performance, the results will come automatically. And if they do not, then you have to find new ways to improve performance. It is at the level of the crucial details in particular that performance can be boosted, and change is implemented.

Companies can learn from sports and arts, where practicing the crucial details is indispensable. In business, there has been a tendency to consider a company's resources, people and machinery, as static elements that make up its production apparatus. Due to the fourth Industrial Revolution or, as we also define it, the 1st Digital Revolution, an increasing number of functions will be taken over by intelligent machines and software. As a consequence, human performance may be what differentiates a company from its competitors. The difference between companies will be their ability to unlock human potential to reinvent organizations and reach higher levels of performance.

A number of companies have professional talent development programs, but not many companies work systematically to unleash human potential and increase performance by empowering teams to find the best ways to reach an ambitious dream.

In sports and the arts, there are designated practices and training times to go over all the things that will occur in a competition or during a performance. In business, most organizations find themselves always playing a critical match – every quarter. Training seldom takes place in closed sessions, and mistakes can have severe consequences. As a consequence, companies are not spending enough efforts training for the next season. As leaders, we must reconsider how we view training and development of human potential – and find ways to unleash human potential, in particular in times of radical change.

To perform optimally in sports and arts, you need to work diligently to get the most out of the roles, the skills and the collaboration. The dream creates the will and working on the details strengthens the critical capabilities of the team.

Once the dream is in place, we start working with the details that need improvements to fulfill it. What players and roles should the team have, what should they be able to do, and what do they need to develop and how should they play together?

We then establish a training routine that allows individual players to develop the skills required for their specific roles. There is a big focus on individual training, even though you coach a team sport. In parallel with developing individuals, we work with the team's game philosophy, i.e., how the team should play and how collaboration between the individuals should work. The training of the details is thus a mix of individually-oriented physical and technical exercises combined with team training focused on tactical elements and collaboration.

It is important that we continually align our routine to ensure that the details are being developed at the highest possible speed. In order to do this, it is important to make improvements and adjustments along the way. The players are not just static pieces of machinery, but people with potential and it is our job as leaders to help them develop.

In business, the training regime is different, but the thinking is the same: How do we create room for development and training of the crucial details so that we can improve our performance? How do we ensure that there is constant focus on performance where it matters and not just the results compared to theoretical plans?

The difference between managing results and managing performance is particularly clear here. If the dream is inspiring, those involved will want to improve their performance, both as individuals and as a team. The desire to improve is a strong motivating force for most people, especially when they find personal meaning in what they are doing. When they also get help to develop along the way, it creates a cycle of affirmation in which they will want to do even more.

If we manage results based on predetermined plans, however, we risk locking employees into predefined tasks which limited potential. On the other hand, if focus is on performance and collaboration, everyone will work to improve it, which can yield far better results than any plan could have imagined.

This way of looking at training affects the way we think about business in general. It affects our leadership, especially as team leaders, and it will affect the way employees see themselves and their colleagues. Improving performance is prioritized over results, because when we improve performance, we can change the company's ambition and help create new opportunities and perform well in the next season.

Bill Walsh put together a 'Standard of Performance,' which is simple but useful advice for leaders who want to work with performance:

- Exhibit a ferocious and intelligently-applied work ethic directed at continual improvement.
- Demonstrate respect for each person in the organization.
- Be deeply committed to learning and teaching, including your own expertise.
- Be fair.
- Demonstrate character.
- Honor the direct connection between details and improvement, relentlessly seek the latter.
- Show self-control, especially under pressure.
- Demonstrate and prize loyalty.
- Use positive language and have a positive attitude.
- Take pride in my effort as an entity separate from the result of that effort.
- Be willing to go the extra distance for the organization.

- Deal appropriately with victory and defeat, adulation and humiliation.
- Promote internal communication that is both open and substantive.
- Seek poise in myself and those I lead.
- Put the team's welfare and priorities ahead of my own.
- Maintain an ongoing level of concentration and focus that is abnormally high.
- Make sacrifice and commitment the organization's trademark.

MEASURE PERFORMANCE

Part of working with details is measuring whether performance of the crucial details is improving. When you manage based on outcomes, it may even be counterproductive to the reinvention of your business. If the future business model cannibalizes the current business, results may worsen during the transition from the old to the new season. We must measure what we are doing and our ability to improve performance, so we can ensure that we increase our ability to perform in the new season.

At SAP, we measured how much time the development team used on innovation, and we measured the speed of development work. With the introduction of Agile, our 20,000 developers could spend more of their time innovating with customers. In addition, innovation projects became faster. As a result, SAP delivered more innovations to their customers in less time. This in turned created a foundation for increased revenue and higher margins.

In other words, we are not against measurements, but we must measure the right things: the improvement of performance within the crucial details, the leading indicators. Used correctly, measurements can tell you whether the critical capabilities and subsequent performance is improving.

In the world of sports, you try to precisely measure all quantitative and qualitative parameters to distinguish performance from the results. You can win a match even if you did not perform well, as long as your opponent was worse, or you were lucky. The results tell you something about the competition but less about your performance, although in more individual sports there is greater consistency between results and performance measurements.

In a team sport, there are countless parameters that tell you something about performance. It may be the number of ball touches, whether the ball is hit accurately, the number of balls won, etc. Together they give a picture of the team's capabilities and provide a basis for assessing where there is potential for improvement. In international matches, it is often small margins that make the difference, and therefore the team with the best performance in the critical areas will most often win.

The final result of a match never tells the whole story. In a sport like soccer, one team can perform far better than the other and yet lose the match due to a random counter attack or an unwarranted penalty kick.

This can also happen in business. Completely random and unforeseeable events can occur and cause poor results, even though performance has been good. If the company solely measures itself on the results, this may be demotivating for employees and it may not inspire the full potential of the team. The underlying circumstances must always be part of the communication around the results. The numbers do not always speak for themselves, so we as leaders need to investigate and understand the real value of numbers and use them to improve performance in the details that matter the most.

RECOMMENDATIONS FOR MEASURING PERFORMANCE

- Define relevant leading indicators to evaluate performance within the crucial details. Measure performance so that it makes sense. Don't just measure results.
- Analyze why performance is not developing as expected. The explanation may lie in several places at the detail level. Spend time with employees to understand how performance is best developed.
- Assess whether the details and performance have improved so much that you can adjust to a more ambitious level.
- Be brutally honest about measurements. Honesty is the basis for improving performance.
- Look for information between the numbers – what are the reason for a current value? What is the whole story about the real value of numbers? Understand the root causes and improve.
- When you evaluate an employee based on numbers, make sure it is specific to the relative task. Respect the current situation experienced by the employee, so that the evaluation creates identified meaning-driven motivation and engagement.
- Make sure everyone understands where the company is improving performance and where it needs further improvements.

CHAPTER 8

THE PLATFORM FOR CHANGE

When the founder of Amazon, Jeff Bezos, bought the renowned American newspaper, The Washington Post, in 2013, most of the media industry was in shock. What would that mean? The newspaper had, like so many other traditional media outlets, declining readership, although the newspaper still made profits due to its leadership cutting costs. Competition from digital media was intense, and The Washington Post had not managed to get ahead economically.

Today the newspaper is profitable. Bezos has hired more employees and invested in serious journalism and digitalization. According to Bezos, the success is due to a shift in focus from advertisers to readers. He emphasizes that a company cannot save its way to greatness. It needs to invest in the future. He had emphasized from the outset that, despite his vast fortune, he doesn't want to be perceived as a philanthropist or sponsor. The worst he could have done was to let the newspaper spend money without considering the profitability. Constraints drive innovation, says Jeff Bezos.

A mindset aimed at the reader and a framework with clear constraints. That is part of the platform for change that Jeff Bezos has created to support the dream and the development of the details. Consider the two components on which the platform is built – the mindset and the framework. The mindset is mainly connected to the dream. What do we need to keep in mind when we make decisions on the job to best achieve the dream? The Washington Post's mindset was "the reader comes first."

The framework, on the other hand, relates mainly to the details. The roles, the skills and the collaboration need to be set free within the framework, which is the company's way of organizing itself, its governance model and the conditions, economic and otherwise, it is subject to.

The mindset helps ensure that the dream is included in all decisions without having to think about it. The framework makes it possible to develop the details optimally to improve performance.

The framework is, by definition, limiting because some conditions are not negotiable, but ideally it supports the reinvention process. Because as Bezos says, the right constraints, i.e., framework, drives innovation. It can also create a sense of security and clarity if the framework is visible and makes sense. For example, imagine a game with constantly changing rules, and you are not told what they are. That would not be efficient because no one knows where to move to, who to play with or how they score points. However, if the framework is well defined, everyone knows the rules and the players can maximize their potential and develop their abilities to increase performance.

The mindset and the framework are the two elements of the platform for change in our leadership model. The mindset translates the dream into decisions and the framework puts the crucial details into action in the right way. The platform ensures that the dream and details are connected at all times, draw inspiration from each other, increase the company's current strengths and accelerate the reinvention process.

MINDSET – THE FILTER FOR THE BRAIN

Consider the example from earlier about driving from A to B. If you are told that you need to do the task with safety in mind, you will comply with all traffic rules, and in a situation where you could pass another vehicle, you might choose to be on the safe side and refrain from passing. If you are told instead to drive from A to B as fast as possible, you would choose to drive more hazardously, perhaps breaking rules along the way and when in doubt, prioritizing speed over safety.

The task is the same, but the mindset is different and that is crucial to which decisions you make on the way.

You could say that the mindset is like a filter for the brain, which determines how to transform the dream into decisions. The filter needs to be aligned with the dream and needs to be installed throughout the organization to ensure consistency. As such, the mindset needs to be easy to understand and remember. A long value statement with a laundry list of supporting points is not going to work.

As mentioned earlier, in sports, the mindset defines how we intend to play the game. How we need to prepare and practice in order to reach a level of play that suits our ambition and dream. Many coaches compare it with having a game philosophy that is closely linked to the level set by their ambitions and dreams.

If all employees share the mindset that the customer's health comes first, as with Wegmans Food Markets, or that the reader is the center of attention, as with The Washington Post, then all employees are likely to make the right decisions to fulfill the dream in moments of doubt, assuming they have the needed competencies to execute the decisions and the right framework to act within.

SAP's historic success was based on the ability to develop software to solve complex business problems. Quite understandably, the company culture had an underlying enthusiasm for complexity, and there was an assumption that the more complex the software was, the more valuable it was for the customer.

This was both right and wrong. Customers, on the one hand, enjoyed the value of having solutions for managing their complex business challenges. On the other hand, users were at times overwhelmed by the complexity of the software. The ability to make complex solutions had created the world's leading ERP business. Now, in order to reinvent the company, complexity stood in the way of a future with easy-to-use, cloud-based mobile solutions.

If SAP was going to reinvent itself and deliver on the dream, everything would have to be simplified. Not only the installation and implementation of software, but the end-user experience especially. In other words, there was a need to translate the ambition of becoming the market leader in cloud computing into a new mindset that could guide all employees towards simplicity and ease-of-use when developing future products.

After a great deal of thought and discussions, we decided to communicate a goal of reaching one billion users using our software by 2015. The target was both provocative and relevant. Provocative because at that time, in 2010, it had taken us 38 years to get to 50 million users.

A goal of getting 950 million more users in only five years was controversial and made everyone who heard it stop and think: could it possibly be done?

At the same time, it was a relevant goal, because it was connected with our company purpose: "We make the world run better and improve people's lives." For the dream to be credible, SAP would have to reach many more people. Not just 10, 20 or even 100 percent more, but radically many more.

We could have chosen a traditional path and determined what would be realistic based on historic figures. With that kind of thinking, 60 million users would have been a relevant target. Instead, we decided to challenge assumptions and reverse the question: if we are to reach a billion users in five years, what do we need to do differently? How do we best become relevant to so many people?

Most importantly, the goal to reach a billion people created the right mindset internally. Software developers in particular responded with enthusiasm: "Wow, imagine if I can create something that can be used by a billion people! That would be cool!"

The immediate enthusiasm was followed up with relevant reflections like: "In order to reach so many users, the software must be intuitive and easy to use." Another realization was: "It's only possible to reach so many people if we can reach them through their mobile devices." This was a sign that the new mindset was about to be born in the company and began to influence the decisions of the teams. A mindset that suited the strategic direction and challenged the assumption in the company that complexity was good.

The old mindset was based on an assumption that complexity was a valued quality. It had been true in the old season, but for SAP's reinvention, success depended on reaching significantly more users than before. Simplicity was a prerequisite. If your mindset is to reach a billion people, then your products obviously have to be simple to access and use. They also have to be so desirable that a billion people would want to use them. The new mindset changed decisions in the self-organized teams – without instructions from management or lengthy detailed specifications.

ASSUMPTIONS MUST BE CHALLENGED

In a season change, when leaders have to create a new mindset, the main question is: What assumptions that were previously right are no longer relevant? As mentioned in the previous chapter about assumptions, they are difficult to challenge. Similar to assessing which roles or skills are no longer relevant, you must also consider the ways of thinking that create obstacles to achieving the dream in the new season.

The next question is: What new assumptions are needed to succeed in the new season? How will the company become a significant and relevant player in future markets? What must your company be able to do, and how is it different from what it does today? At SAP, the most important new assumption was that simplicity and speed are crucial to achieving the dream.

From there, you can work on defining a new mindset to guide the decision-making process in the company in the right direction – aligned with the dream. Ask yourself: "What narrative would ensure that all involved intuitively make decisions that best lead to the fulfillment of the dream?"

A mindset must not be a fixed procedure that dictates every decision. Many companies have procedures for how things should be handled, such as customer complaints. A procedure or rule of thumb is not the same as a mindset. A mindset reminds people what is important to keep in mind when making decisions.

The mindset has to be clear and at the same time allow employees to use their judgment. An employee may find a much better solution than the one planned in advance in a procedure. The American retail chain, Nordstrom, is known for their customer service and their most important message to employees is: "Use your best judgment in all situations."

Symbolic acts can help make the mindset clear. When Thomas Borgen, as new director for Danske Bank, abolished the drivers and special cafeteria for the executive team, it was a symbolic act stressing the mindset that the bank was for all and not just the elite.

Installing a specific mindset to translate the dream into day-to-day decisions close to the action is one of the most powerful ways to unleash human potential in an organization that needs to reinvent itself.

RECOMMENDATIONS FOR THE MINDSET

- Assess which of your company's assumptions are obsolete in relation to the future market and the company's dream.
- Define a new assumption which is crucial for reaching the dream and creating maximum change in everyday habits and decisions.
- Translate the future assumption to a motto that gives employees the right mindset for their day-to-day decision making.

- Make sure that everyone understands the philosophy of "the game to be developed and played" and what kind of mindset and subsequent behavior that it demands.
- Live by the new mindset. Communicate, explain and illustrate it.
- Be sure to show the new mindset in action. Remember that you are the role model everyone will observe.

THE FRAMEWORK – THE OPTIMAL COURT TO PLAY ON

The mindset translates the dream into day-to-day decisions. The other part of platform, the framework, is a set of conditions and boundaries that the company needs to operate within. The framework contains all conditions within which a company works. It includes external conditions like legislation, compliance rules, standards, regulations, etc., as well as internal conditions like organizational structures, operating models, decision structures, remuneration models and code of conduct.

In the world of sports, it is about the field we play on, the rules we have to follow to play the game and the objective of the game to win. Because all players know the rules and the objective of the game, they are able to perform without spending time debating the rules. The clarity of the rules allows the players to focus on their performance and ensures clear consequences when someone breaks the rules. Besides the rules of the game, the framework in sports also includes the methods under which we train and models for how we work with each other to improve performance.

In training, it is critical to unlock the potential of the team. If you want to be competitive with the best teams in the world, you always have to look at these teams to benchmark how they train and develop as players. We constantly ask ourselves the question: "Could we increase the amount of training and optimize opportunities to develop our capabilities? "

In retrospect, our development philosophy regarding the framework could be explained in the following way: We worked with new training methods daily, so the players were constantly pushed to improve. Some worked better than others did, but new paths were constantly explored. This included special video recordings and computer analyses that were unique at the time. We did exercises in which we focused solely on the quality of the technical execution, and where the results were not important. We did that to ensure that the qualitative progress came first, which would improve results down the road. Often, changing a technique would hamper results in the short term, but if the technique was improved, then we would see better results in the long run. It required courage and patience.

The players were involved in giving each other feedback on the quality of their technical performances and worked as each other's coaches. Not only did they help each other, but their own progress was also strengthened.

Every training session had its focus and the technical training became especially nerdy. We dug deep to get an understanding of what could help the individual player. It turned out that these personal sessions where the individual was the focus were immensely important for the players and the team.

Even midway through a season, we still had projects centered on the constant improvement of the details for an individual player, which was one of the great sources of motivation. It was clear that this was the primary source of meaning for the players, and it also created self-esteem and respect for individuals within the team.

It was not just about being part of a winning team or being part of the starting lineup in the matches. It was about an environment that appreciated each player's development and celebrated their new abilities. That was what created the team spirit and gave us a better chance of winning.

Without knowing, the inspiration for the framework we used was the Self Determination Theory developed by Richard M. Ryan and

Edward L. Deci. It explains why our environment and model had been so effective by recognizing competence, autonomy and belonging. All those factors had been central in our handling of the individual player. Many things in this period also went wrong, and many players would probably say, "Yes, but that is not what always happened." And that's correct, but we always tried to do our best. Many decisions were intuitive but turned out to be right, now that we look back at it.

The key to working with organizations and teams is to work with individuals. It is all about finding out what is meaningful to the individual. It is about finding the meaning, whether it is for someone who works independently or is a part of a team or large organization.

We created a tradition that was honored as a special code of conduct. We agreed that the first practice after we had won a championship would be the hardest of the year. This signaled that: "We won, so now everyone else will work even harder to defeat us in the future. So today we take another significant step forward – it is a new season, and it starts today."

The annual framework to improve the details became the path we all followed. It was our shared path to development. The framework could not be waived. In the rare case that a player could not make it to practice, they would always, through the coach, inform the team of the reason. And the reason had to be accepted by everyone on the team. We depended on each other and each other's abilities. We were a team, and if we lost faith in each other, it would undermine our shared dream. That couldn't happen.

All practices started and ended with a line-up or briefing. At line-up, we always hit on common themes and narratives to inspire the team. Where we were on our common journey, and what was the next exciting destination? Could we open new doors to a new arena tomorrow? A line-up also involved clear direction of what each individual would get out of the practice. What was the purpose of this specific practice? If not articulated clearly, motivation would not be brought up to the level that the unique project required. It was demanding both physically and mentally and required extraordinary commitment from the players and their families.

In business, personal coaching is often limited to an annual performance review with each employee. The review usually includes calculating the bonus for the previous year and defining the development areas of the next year. Imagine if business leaders would implement the framework of sports and coach individuals on a continuous basis. It would accelerate the development of the human potential in the organization and make the annual talk irrelevant. Imagine the impact such a framework would have on performance.

The framework in business is often focused on external rules. The external rules are often very clear and so are the consequences. However, in many companies, employees feel a lack of clarity or consequence around the internal framework. It is a bit like standing on a soccer field in dense fog – you can only see the closest markings. You don't have a feel for the field as a whole, so you stay within your range of sight, and can't see where you are going. You might be in the right position, but your ability to perform is limited. Professor Jan Molin from Copenhagen Business School explains that when the big picture is unclear, individual actions often seem meaningless and irrelevant. If an employee has a hard time seeing the big picture, the cohesion within the organization crumbles, even if some individuals strive to do the right thing. The reaction from management is often to try to control the situation even more by making goals and performance requirements even more specific, but that just makes it even harder for the individual to see and understand their role in the big picture.

We believe it is important to be very clear on the big picture and the framework within which the company operates. This clarity allows for freedom to make decisions and perform without concerns.

You can adjust the framework so it continuously supports the best possible performance at a given point in time. But adjustments must be explained well and understood by everyone, otherwise people will begin to doubt the fairness of the game and become unengaged.

THE FRAMEWORK MUST MAKE SENSE

As mentioned, it is important that the framework supports the dream and the work on the details. The framework is not a goal, but a tool. The framework is based on and defined by the strategic direction of your company. Many leaders have announced a reorganization as part of a transformation project. The reorganization may have been relevant, but if the reasons for the change of framework was not explained well, it may have been perceived as an unfair change. Others have been involved in change projects designed to rally employees around a new strategic direction of the company, and experienced enthusiasm in the beginning. But the enthusiasm slowly faded because the framework was not changed to support the new direction. Inconsistencies between what we say and what people experience every day can kill any change effort.

It might be because the mindset in a company contradicts the dream. If the company says one thing and does something else, the credibility of the dream disappears. Often, a company's organizational structure is the obstacle. Think of the IBM example, in which Lou Gerstner wanted to be more focused on customer needs. It would have been an obstacle and made the dream pointless if IBM had kept a structure based on geography or products. Instead, they implemented a new structure based on global industry solution units that allowed the organization to be closer to their customers and develop a better understanding of their needs and how to serve them best. This was fully in line with their dream to become a leading services company.

WHO SHOULD PLAY ON THE SAME TEAM?

The most important question when creating the framework is: "Who should play on the same team?"

If software developers are to work closely with product designers, they should not be sitting too far apart. Perhaps they should not be split up in different departments or even in different rooms.

At SAP, that was the conclusion we came to after deciding to introduce Agile development methods. The structure was previously based on specialization, which fit with the old assumption that complexity was good. But when SAP changed seasons, simplicity and speed was necessary, so the key roles had to work together in teams instead of in silos. The organizational structure was changed from specialized, hierarchical structures to self-organized teams.

At the same time, the role of management changed. When the Agile process works, the self-organized teams become self-regulating. Because of this, management tasks changed radically. Instead of planning, deciding and measuring, management's role was to coach team members, develop team skills, and eliminate impediments.

The change meant that we could substantially reduce the number of organizational levels and middle managers, as the self-organized Agile teams no longer needed control beyond what the product owner and the Scrum master delivered. The transformation of middle managers' roles was the biggest obstacle to overcome in the transformation, because it challenged the power structure within the organization. However, many of the middle managers were subsequently given roles closer to the product or customers and experienced increased satisfaction because they were part of a more meaningful process of direct value creation.

It was important to determine that there is no one-size-fits-all formula. Self-governing teams may be right to achieve one dream, but not the optimal framework for another. Some companies may need to have some roles close together, while others in cross-departmental teams. The important thing is removing the obstacles preventing optimal collaboration and change. If there are constant conflicts between two departments, it may indicate that the framework has not found its optimal form. However, it may also be a sign that the framework is not sufficiently visible for all so the role distribution and expectations for collaboration are unclear. That will create uncertainty and a breeding ground for conflict.

TRANSPARENCY AND VISIBILITY

As mentioned above, the framework should be visible for everyone, so they are able to see the entire field and know who is playing where and which roles depend on each other. Even if you only play a small role, your ability to perform increases if you can see the big picture and know how what you do fits into the bigger scheme of things. It increases motivation and improves collaboration.

Visibility and transparency around the framework create a sense of confidence. Autonomy increases, and people have freedom to develop within the framework. We believe it makes sense for a company to increase employees' sense of empowerment. Often it is the employees who are in close contact with customers or products, who know the company's situation best and how it can improve. Digitalization further contributes to transparency and knowledge sharing. Keep in mind that empowerment does not mean "do whatever you want." A precondition for increasing empowerment is that the dream and mindset are shared by everyone and that the framework is clear to everyone.

When all the employees in an organization understand the dream and develop their own and the organization's performance on the important details, they will begin to make improvement proposals on their own. The role of the leader changes from making crucial decisions to asking relevant questions. The answers will come from employees.

It requires everyone to understand where the company is in relation to the dream and how the capabilities within crucial details are improving. Communication plays a critical role here.

CALIBRATING THE FRAMEWORK

To simplify how you can work with and calibrate the framework, imagine a playing field in sports. The mindset is what the game strategy is about – how do we play to win? The framework is the markings on the field and the rules that must be followed in the game. On the field, the players must use their roles and skills and collaborate to move in the direction of the dream, as individuals and as a team.

A coach cannot control every move on the field since the game moves too fast, but the coach can make sure everyone has the same mindset – the game strategy. A coach can also make sure that the field and the rules are clear to everyone. And a coach can make sure that the crucial details have been trained sufficiently. Through these interventions the coach ensures that the players can unleash their full potential as a team and increases the likelihood of achieving the dream. Imagine the impact on the performance, if it is unclear where the field is or if team members are uncertain about whether or not they are allowed to pick up the ball and run with it.

Some coaches will try to control everything from the sidelines, but it is far less effective than preparing the team and training to play the game in the best possible way. This ability is enabled through an ambitious dream, a common mindset, a distinct framework and training in the details that matter most. In sports this is quite clear. Are we as clear about this in business?

Clarity and consistency are keys to success. A leader has to calibrate the framework so that it creates optimal conditions for teams to perform. Does the framework give maximum freedom to act without weakening the direction and ambition? Is the framework visible and understood? Is the framework productive and does it allow the team to unleash their full potential?

As the team develops and reaches new levels of performance, the framework may need adjustments. In times of radical change due to a season change, the framework needs to be recalibrated quite frequently as the organization moves from the old to the new season. In periods of less change, the challenge is preventing the framework from turning into bureaucracy.

Communicating adjustments to the framework is critical. The framework must be trusted by all involved. If it is changed without notice or explanation, it creates insecurity and frustration, which will reduce performance. Instead of focusing on reaching the ambitious dream, people begin to discuss the framework itself. A sign of this is when the organizational structure or internal reporting lines become a main topic at the lunch table.

There are undoubtedly leaders who will insist that it is the employees' own problem to understand the changes and accept the framework, that management's job is not to be a therapist. In our experience, there is no contradiction in paying attention to business results and paying attention to human aspects. The two go hand in hand. To achieve high performance, it is critical for leaders to ensure that all people involved share the same dream, train the important details, work within the boundaries of a common framework and make decisions based on a common mindset. It will be difficult, if not impossible, to achieve high performance if you don't pay sufficient attention to the human factor. After all, the human factor creates the basis of differentiation in most companies and it is the critical ingredient to reinvent the company at high speed.

That is not to say that the company should adapt to every individual's wishes and desires. But when you change the framework, the new framework should be visible and aligned with the dream and accepted by everyone. Leaders should not change the framework without good reason. When the reason for change is aligned with the ambition of the dream and the need to develop the crucial details, people are likely to be inspired by the change and will engage proactively in the next phase of the reinvention.

RECOMMENDATIONS FOR THE FRAMEWORK

- Define a logical framework so it is visible and aligned with the dream and the change phase of the company. Allow freedom to perform within the framework.
- Set up the framework so that it can both optimize the existing season and develop a new season. This may require a temporary framework to protect efforts in the early stage of the new season.
- Remove unnecessary hierarchical levels to ensure that the crucial details are maximized, so that unproductive actions don't undermine the big picture.
- Define future meeting structures and governance models to ensure that new roles and abilities are in place, and collaboration runs smoothly, improving over time.
- Recalibrate the framework as the organization moves to the next level of the reinvention. Make sure there's always an optimal connection between the dream and details. Be clear about and changes and provide thorough explanations of the changes, so it supports and accelerates the speed of reinvention.
- The framework must secure optimal opportunities for unleashing and unfolding the potential of individual employees as well as collaboration within teams and across the organization.

CHAPTER 9

THE BIG PICTURE – A DYNAMIC BALANCING ACT

The National Geographic Society: a name that radiates history. The Society has published magnificent photos and groundbreaking articles from all around the world for more than 100 years. National Geographic is Dian Fossey and her gorillas in the mist, the discovery of the Inca's Machu Picchu in Peru and unknown tribal people of Indonesia. It is the flag on the moon planted by astronauts from the Apollo 11 expedition.

The Society was founded in the United States in 1888 by 33 explorers and scientists wanting to increase the general public's knowledge of geography. They created the magazine, which became one of the world's most famous and respected. Symbolically, the company was founded the same year as the ballpoint pen and Kodak's first handheld camera.

When John Fahey became chief executive in 1998, the monthly magazine was still the Society's main product. A few years before, National Geographic had created their website, published a Japanese sister-magazine and started its own television company. The changes were few and small, following the company's assumption that there was no need for big changes since being a source of information was more important than commercial interests. "It was an organization with lots of history, with its glory days behind it," John Fahey noted later. He found the organization formal and cautious. Decisions took forever, and the attitude of the employees was: "How do I secure my position?" rather than: "What can we achieve."

John Fahey saw the need to bring the National Geographic Society into the global and digital age, and he began a massive restructuring program that fundamentally changed the way the organization conducted business. Over the following ten years, the organization changed from being primarily based on a physical magazine to a multi-platform organization that reached 360 million people globally. The organization created multiple sister products, films, radio programs, music, maps, travel expeditions, educational material, exhibitions and the National Geographic Channel, which became a permanent fixture of almost all cable television providers. The company also branched out into e-commerce, with clothing and garden items, among other things.

The change in National Geographic was, in many ways, typical for a change of season driven by digital transformation, where the traditional physical products and physical customer interactions are challenged by digital platforms and virtual customer relations. Fahey understood that a season change required that all elements of change were calibrated and developed at the same time. The change of strategy required not just a change of the product and business model, but also the culture, compensation structure, organization and people. Even the company's mission was challenged in the process. In 2004, Fahey changed the company's mission from "increase and spread the knowledge of geography" to "inspiring people to take care of the planet."

YOU CANNOT CHEAT THE DREAMS AND DETAILS LEADERSHIP MODEL

In many ways, National Geographic under John Fahey has done what we are recommending: they identified a season change and created a dream that set the direction for National Geographic in a new season, all based on an inspiration anchored in a new purpose. Fahey identified details in new business areas that were crucial to the new season, just as he created an innovative mindset and new framework with room for innovation.

The National Geographic example shows with great clarity that by themselves, the dream, the details and framework are not enough. The parts must be carefully calibrated to work together. If the elements are not calibrated and developed in parallel, then change will not be sustained. Balance and consistency between the elements creates the necessary meaning and develops new potential.

Many times, as leaders, we are too busy to develop all the elements in parallel and therefore chose to focus on the parts that best fit our immediate priorities and can create the biggest change here and now.

However, in order for Dreams and Details leadership to be effective in transforming the organization, it is necessary to ensure that all elements are in balance and support each other. It will quickly be visible if the elements of the model are not balanced.

You can't just develop an inspiring dream and hope that the organization itself will figure out the details, just like you can't assume that the existing mindset and framework will still fit. The parts work together dynamically and an imbalance will reduce their effectiveness and change will be limited and temporary.

You cannot cheat the model. If there is an element missing or misaligned, you must act as a leader. The dream might be inaccurate or insufficiently rooted in the company. The details might not be prioritized correctly. Often the platform is the most obvious place to look for issues. Does your company's mindset and framework support the dream and details, or do they hold the company back due to old assumptions or old habits?

If the model does not logically fit together, the people involved will immediately discover it and a sense of meaninglessness will replace the needed engagement. Everyone must have a feeling that they have a real chance to contribute to the dream and an opportunity to unleash their full potential to achieve the dream.

ADJUSTING THE ELEMENTS CONTINUOUSLY

If National Geographic had continued in 1999 as if nothing had changed, the company would have probably been fighting for its survival a few years later. But by investing in the next season, they developed new business areas and created a foundation for survival in a digital world. However, in 2008, the financial crisis hit all industries, including National Geographic. National Geographic responded in 2009 by dismissing employees and cutting costs in distribution. For John Fahey and the other leaders, it became crucial to determine if the challenges were only due to the financial crisis or more fundamental changes were at stake.

A survey of nearly 500 employees revealed that they were frustrated and found several things meaningless. They complained about territorial struggles between departments, poor conflict management, uncertainty about promotions, inefficient and slow service in many departments and an unclear line of command. The employee survey showed that silo-thinking was dominant, and the many new functional areas had been set up as isolated businesses, which created a competitive atmosphere instead of joint mission for the organization. The issues became very apparent when three departments managed to launch similar national park initiatives within only two weeks.

The challenges in 2009 indicated an urgent need to take the next steps in the reinvention of the company. After a phase of developing new business areas, it was time to focus and integrate the organization again. The inspiration of the dream was common for all, and still clear: "to inspire people to take care of the planet," but the number of different and competing business units indicated that the direction had become blurred and collaboration wasn't working. The fact that Fahey had 14 directors reporting to him at the time indicated that the framework was based on silo structures, which increased uncertainty and imbalance in the model.

The new strategy had some good elements, but it became apparent that the elements and the big picture had not developed concurrently with new opportunities. Instead, competition arose among the existing departments and the new. Each department was more focused on its own success than contributing to the shared dream and collaborating on the details that were essential to the future.

The many new business areas created uncertainty about priorities. What was the core business? How could the different business areas interact with customers in a consistent way? In which areas could the company become exceptionally good to reach the dream? Online content, TV-production or selling merchandise?

The clear signals from employees lead to a comprehensive restructuring, which included an inclusion of a new senior executive position responsible for e-commerce across all divisions. The adjustment of the framework was aimed at increasing collaboration across product divisions, and integrating the various product offerings towards the customer.

The question is whether National Geographic held on to the old framework based on independent product divisions too long. The framework had supported the creation of new opportunities, but later, the framework limited the opportunity to create synergies necessary to reach the full potential of the new purpose. A couple of years later, the company went through the biggest restructuring in its history. Today National Geographic is divided into the National Geographic Society, which is still a non-profit, publishing magazines and in charge of an e-shop, and National Geographic Partners, primarily in charge of the TV programs, which are commercially operated. The latter is a result of 21st Century Fox buying the TV channel in 2015.

The National Geographic example shows the challenge and importance of calibrating the leadership model over time, so all elements are developed in parallel and reinvention is accelerated. In the first phase of a season change, the challenge may be to create room for innovation in new business areas while the existing business is optimized. In the second phase of the season change, the different innovations and independent initiatives may need to be integrated to create synergy and increase value for customers.

One requirement for a successful reinvention of an organization is that the work with the dream, details and the platform is calibrated and balanced. Another condition is that change should be a dynamic process where all elements are developed over time in parallel, so the move to the new season can accelerate and become exponential.

When a company focuses on the details, performance can gradually improve to a point where it is possible to increase ambitions and accelerate new abilities to speed up the change of season. It is this dynamic process that makes the change of season exponential. If the elements are not developed in line with the change, you may risk that development stops or that the elements become unbalanced, as was the case with National Geographic. Therefore, it is important for executives to constantly keep an eye on the development and listen to the organization's reactions and act on them.

For a large company with a lot at stake in the old season, a successful reinvention also requires the ability to optimize its existing business. A fast move to the next season without diligent attention to the existing business could kill the opportunity to reinvent the company. In this respect, it is easier to be a start-up company without any history or legacy to take into account. This is a freedom that larger successful organizations seldom have. That is what Clayton Christensen calls "the innovator's dilemma." We think the dilemma can be solved by combining an evolutionary and revolutionary approach and then gradually accelerating the change of season until it becomes a new way of conducting business.

CONFLICT BETWEEN NEW AND EXISTING

John Fahey managed to reinvent National Geographic and create new platforms while preserving the existing business with its traditions and reputation. But the example also demonstrates that even if Fahey had created a relevant dream and was successful in the first phase of the reinvention, the platform that created the change in the first place later became an inhibitor.

The biggest challenge is to initiate the season change and accelerate it over time until the reinvention is completed. When a company changes season, a natural conflict occurs between existing and new businesses. The deciding factor for a successful season change is the ability to ensure that the shift from existing to the new season takes place at the right speed at the right time. Too much focus on the existing business, with all its weight and inertia, will crush the new season before it even gets started. But if the new season receives too much attention, the existing business may die too quickly, reducing the company's financial strength and the ability to complete the change of season. The leadership challenge is to ensure that the two seasons collaborate based on a joint dream for the future.

The dilemma is similar to the challenge in sports when a team wants to integrate new players in a team of experienced players. You need to make sure that the older players will commit to and take responsibility for the integration of these new players, and be acknowledged for their contribution in creating new stars. If not, they will exclude them, as they see them as competitors, and at the same time become weaker players themselves as time goes by. It will create a war inside the team and will undermine competitiveness.

Many leaders and coaches think that they develop stronger teams by letting the two groups of players compete with each other for the limited positions on the team. But they often realize that it does not lead to an accelerated transition to a new season and greater competitiveness.

This brings us back to the three crucial psychological needs necessary for human beings when it comes to internal meaning-driven motivation and engagement. If you feel threatened, or that your competence is under question and your autonomy is removed, you will feel that it undermines your position in the group. In that case, you will fight to regain your old position.

If instead, you are asked to take responsibility for a new player's development and you are seen as an invaluable part of their success, because you have the competence to play that part, the situation will be different. You will step into the "new role", with a new identity in the group. That new role will be acknowledged and reestablish your feeling of belonging. It will make a lot more sense than competing against the new players in the team.

When the time comes when they take over your position, you will find it natural, and everybody will support the narrative that you were a big contributor to the development of the new talent and reinvention of the team.

The transition between the old and the new is one of the most challenging tasks in leading a reinvention. Your authentic, consistent and consequential leadership is fundamental to solving this dilemma. Displaying authentic inspiration for the dream will create excitement around the transition for everyone – both old and new members of the team. Your personal involvement in the development of the crucial details will create clarity and opportunities for everyone to develop and unleash their potential. And your consistent and consequential handling of resistance creates credibility around the need for change.

CHAPTER 10

SEASON CHANGE – CONNECTING THE OLD AND THE NEW

Seen from above, Manhattan, New York is a marvelous sight, completely different from any other major city in the world. The roads are close together and straight, with avenues going north to south and streets going east to west. But in the middle of it all, the orderly system is broken up by a green oasis: the one-and-a-half square mile Central Park.

On the busy streets and avenues, the pace is fast, and people are focused. People typically look down, at their mobile phones or the pavement, and they rush from one place to another. Whether they are on foot, in a taxi or the subway, time is not to be wasted. It can be exhausting as an outsider if you are dropped in the middle of it, but eventually you get drawn in and become infected with the energy buzzing in the streets.

Compared to the busy streets, Central Park is a completely different world. But the park is just as important to New York and the city's pulse and identity as the densely-packed streets and avenues. In Central Park, people are not as busy or focused. They play and talk, laugh, love and reflect. There is time to just look up at the trees and the sky. The atmosphere in the park is one for enjoying, not performing. It's a place to be free and let the mind wander, where the hectic pace slows for a while.

Creative ideas rarely come to life in the busy streets and avenues. Creativity may begin to grow in the daily bustle, but it is only when there is time to think and interact with others that it really blossoms.

In the streets and avenues, people usually know exactly where they are going. In Central Park, they stroll along without a fixed purpose and interact with people they wouldn't normally meet. This often creates unanticipated connection points that can lead to new and original ideas. Or, in Steve Jobs' words: "There's a temptation in our networked age to think that ideas can be developed by email and iChat. That's crazy. Creativity comes from spontaneous meetings, from random discussions. You run into someone, you ask what they're doing, you say 'wow,' and soon you're cooking up all sorts of ideas."

Unfortunately, many companies have paved over Central Park to get more streets and avenues. Others restrict Central Park to a particular department that is allowed to be creative, such as marketing or research and development. Creativity has been cut to a minimum, and it is frowned upon to just hang out at informal meeting places or around the water cooler.

As leaders, we do not need to create a physical park, but it is important to create a space where people can think freely and meet with others without necessarily having a specific purpose. And it should not be just for the few people who work in a specific department. Everyone must have access to Central Park, and it can't be a closed-off reservation where its residents cannot come out and be part of the energetic bustle of streets and where the inhabitants of the busy streets cannot go to gain inspiration and new ideas.

There are many reasons for a company to create a creative oasis when attempting to reinvent. People improve performance more when there is time and space for creativity and new thoughts after a busy period. We are not creative when we run at top speed at all times. Also, having an opportunity to meet informally with people in other roles and departments builds trust across the organization. When we trust each other, we feel free to present new thoughts and ideas, and when we talk together, we learn more about the problems and challenges others have, and can collaborate on how to solve them. A company's dream and mindset often are cultivated in the park, where there is time to remind ourselves why we do what we do, reflect on and challenge assumptions and come up with ideas for improvements and new ways of working.

For companies who want to reinvent from a position of strength, work being done in the current season is best managed in the streets and avenues. You optimize existing processes and make improvements. Reinvention is often initiated in Central Park. A company's Central Park is not just for pleasure and informal meetings, it is also the place where new thoughts develop and assumptions are challenged. However, everyone should be able to contribute, whether they work with the current or the coming season.

Central Park is not better than the streets and avenues and vice versa. It is necessary to be efficient and focused. Likewise, it is necessary to challenge assumptions, come up with new ideas and meet informally. As leaders, we must lead in both the park and the streets and the interaction between them.

TRAINING AND MATCHES AT THE SAME TIME

The Central Park analogy applies to the world of sports as well. In sports, there are dedicated times for training. In fact, most of the time is consumed by training. Training enables higher performance in matches. In training, the conditions are like Central Park, where new ideas can be tested, developed and refined without great risk. Most of the time is spent in training, so you can play your best during a match. This would be difficult in an established company, where it is not possible to take a training break for a quarter or two. Companies must be able to optimize their existing business, i.e., matches, while at the same time training for or experimenting in a new season.

In many companies, training is limited to the research and development departments, where staff experiment with new ideas for the future. However, input for these experiments should come from the entire company as well as from outside the company. The biggest difference between training and matches is that it is ok to make mistakes while training. In the training phase, investments in experiments are small, and they must be guided by a "fail fast or scale fast" approach. This takes the stress out of failing and turns it into learning moments instead. Experiments must first and foremost challenge existing assumptions and be used to test new ideas.

The most difficult job during training is choosing what experiments to prioritize in the new season. Not all experiments can be included in the new season, so in many ways it becomes a process of deselection. It takes courage to pick specific experiments and gamble on their success, and even more courage to reject and stop projects. But it is vital to effectively change season. Similarly, in sports, new elements of the game developed during training are not implemented into a game plan until they are known to substantially increase the team's competitiveness in match situations.

Once the selections and rejections have been made, leadership changes focus. It moves towards building credibility around the new approach and maximize scale. This phase requires less focus on experiments and a significantly greater focus on scaling the crucial details – often new skills and new ways of working.

A change of season occurs when the right ideas and projects are scaled, and the new details are developed and become part of the existing business. This is how the company reinvents itself, and the process can start over again.

The dynamic process from experimentation and ideation to scale and integration can be illustrated as an exponential curve with different phases.

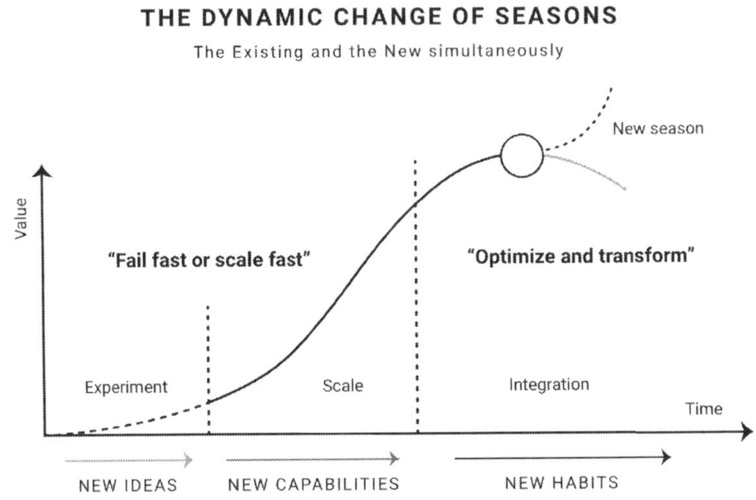

Figure 5: A Dynamic Season Change

As illustrated in the figure, the company consists of a combination of the existing business and initiatives for a new season going on concurrently. The new season is created through two stages – "Experiment" and "Development". In the early stages, experiments explore new ideas. It is a phase with rapid iterations and high risk of failure. The ideas must be either discarded quickly, or moved on to the next phase, where they will be developed. The reinvention of the company takes place in three steps: the selection of the right ideas, the accelerated scale and the integration of the new skills into new best practices or habits in the existing business.

INTRODUCING THE NEW SEASON

A start-up company works exclusively in the new season. However, this is not the case for an established company that is primarily focused on serving existing customers and competing with existing competitors. Some will say that it's easier to create a new season as a startup because it is not distracted by the habits and traditions of the existing business. This may be true, but if you can create the right balance between the existing and the new season, it can be a great advantage to have an existing well-functioning business.

Many startups spend a lot of time trying to get access to the capital needed to scale in the new season, whereas established companies often have the necessary financial strength to invest in the next season. This adds an advantage over startups. In addition to access to capital and resources, established companies benefit from having recognizable brands, established customer relationships and access to global markets.

In spite of this, start-up companies often win the race to the new season. They react more quickly to the new rules of the new season than established companies limited by bureaucracy, slowness, wrong assumptions or old habits. Therefore, the task of leaders in established companies during a season change is to ensure that the company does not slow down in the face of change, but act at a startup while at the same time leveraging their strength, reach and scale.

TRAINING – THE NEW SEASON

The vast majority of the ideas in the experimental phase will be discarded, but once it is clear that an idea has potential to transform the industry, the project should move to the next phase, in which it will be developed and scaled. At this point, the company must act as a startup in many ways.

Traditionally, the opportunity to develop new ideas is reviewed through an investment plan. The starting point for an investment plan is typically the expected return on invested capital for the investment opportunity.

In a season change, this unfortunately means that companies often will have a tendency to over-invest in the existing business and underinvest in future business. This is because the existing business provides a known, stable return and is perceived as less risky. In addition, returns in new areas will often be uncertain, and the company has limited experience in the new area. It is very rare that a leader will ask the relevant question: "What is the risk of *not* investing in something new?"

Once the decision about what to invest in is made, the next challenge is to scale the new project as quickly as possible. This phase requires leaders to create the best possible conditions for growth and development of the new approach. An important responsibility of leadership is to build credibility for new initiatives and protect them from old assumptions or habits. It's a bit like an acorn, which could grow into a giant oak tree, but stays in the shadow of other big trees and therefore does not have good growing conditions, unless it gets special attention.

In this case, leaders need to identify limitations to scaling the new season and remove them. One significant limitation is that the new project often challenges the existing season and is potentially perceived as a threat to current business. Therefore, there will naturally be resistance to new projects, and many will claim that they make no sense. Leaders must protect the new projects and make sure that early signs of success are visible so that the projects are given ample opportunity to develop.

Some companies choose to run these new projects externally. There may be good reasons for doing this, but we should note that it makes it much more difficult to integrate the new season into the established organization later. You risk that the season change takes place outside of the company, developing at its own pace like a speedboat, and leaving the existing company floundering like a massive inflexible ship adrift in the old season. So, it's important that the speedboat can also be a tugboat that stays tethered to the mother ship and can help it navigate faster to a new season.

It is often crucial for success in the development phase that the project is led by a proven but open-minded leader from the existing business. This increases credibility and helps integrate new abilities into the daily workings of the existing business.

OPTIMIZING – ENABLING THE NEW SEASON

While some parts of the business are experimenting with new opportunities in the training room, the existing organization needs to continue to optimize in the current season. In other words, the established part of the company needs to focus on improving and streamlining existing processes in the current season in order to release capital and resources that can be invested in the next season. To prevent the existing company from overpowering the experiments in the new season, the two areas are often separated. This is what Fahey did at National Geographic when he created several new parallel businesses to find new opportunities. However, the risk is that the existing company does not become part of the season change and those involved do not feel that they are contributing to the reinvention.

To avoid this, you must make it clear to everyone that the existing company is enabling the funding of the new season through its ability to increase efficiencies in the current business. In addition, the existing business plays an important role in integrating the new capabilities into the business when the time is right to change season. Therefore, it is crucial that the company is working on the same dream – direction, ambition and inspiration – so it becomes the unifying element for the whole company and not just for a part of it. The employees in the existing business must know that they are as crucial to fulfilment of the dream as those involved in the new season. Being able to transfer new skills to the existing business is critical for a successful reinvention.

It is a cyclical process, where leadership disciplines used will vary in the different parts of your business. Some areas need to be optimized, while other areas will be scaled back, and space for experiments and learning needs to be created. Therefore, it is important to evaluate the existing company and the new season separately because they need to be assessed based on different criteria.

Performance criteria in the existing company should be focused on efficiency, continuous improvement and development of new capabilities, while performance in the new season should be measured in terms of speed, new capabilities and growth. By separating how you measure performance in different areas of the business, you can better assess how far along the reinvention has progressed and adjust elements of the leadership model as the company moves into exponential growth in the new season.

EVERYONE CONTRIBUTES TO THE SEASON CHANGE

Reinvention requires demands that we, as leaders, clearly communicate how everyone is contributing, and that everyone is important. If part of the business is no longer important, it's better to cut it off, rather than ignore it. This creates clarity for everyone.

Employees in the existing business will typically want clarity about their future. It is important to address this. It is absolutely essential to inspire all employees in the company to rally around the dream and the future. Different parts of the company play different roles, and they develop and change over time. As the new season unfolds, more and more employees working in the existing business will participate in the new season and develop new skills and take on new roles. As a result, the new season gradually becomes part of the existing business, completing the reinvention, and allowing the search for the next season.

THE BOARD OF DIRECTORS IN A NEW SEASON

Developing the right dream and working with the crucial details to reinvent the company is a daily task for the executive team. The board of directors is not directly involved in this work. Nevertheless, the board of directors in a modern company can play an important role in creating space for executives to reinvent the company.

The board of directors traditionally spends most of its time reviewing the company's financial performance in the current season. Boards typically meet quarterly to ensure that quarterly results are satisfactory, and the company is compliant with legislative regulations and other requirements. As a result, most of their time is focused on historical efforts and results. The quarterly results are typically compared to the budget to assess whether the company is performing as planned. But the comparison with the budget tells us mostly about how good the executive team has been at planning – and not so much about how the company is performing in the market, and even less about the progress of the reinvention

Quarterly results are also compared to last year's results. This is a more relevant comparison, as it tells us something about how the company has developed since last year. However, it still does not tell how it is developing the next season. Many boards also spend time assessing the company's results in relation to competitors. This is a much more relevant analysis, but here too, you risk comparing yourself to traditional competitors, which all play according to the rules of the game in the old season.

Often, boards spend too little time assessing new competitors, usually because such competitors often are relatively small and unknown companies. However, if a competitor is growing more than 50 percent per year, it doesn't matter how big they are. They may have found a new way of providing value to customers that challenges the rules of the game in the next season. Therefore, it makes sense for executives and the board to understand what they are doing differently that could create new opportunities for the company.

Unless there is a major crisis in the existing business, the board should spend ample time understanding the coming seasons and help ensure sufficient investments have been made to create new opportunities. In a time of radical change, one of the board's greatest responsibilities should be to ensure that the company has a viable future.

MANAGING RISK IS ALSO ABOUT TAKING RISK

In addition to evaluating quarterly financial statements, a company's board assesses potential risks the company is facing. Risk management is an important task to ensure shareholder value over time. However, the task must not become an exercise in *avoiding* risk. In a season change, a tendency to not take risks may be the greatest risk of all of them.

The role of the board of directors has evolved significantly in recent years. Traditionally, the main job of the board was compliance, i.e., that the company acts in accordance with applicable laws, rules and regulations. Over the past few years, corporate governance requirements have risen sharply, partly due to the financial crisis in 2008 and a number of corporate scandals where companies and managers have not handled their responsibilities properly. Therefore, the task of ensuring compliance is significant and, in many ways, the board sets the tone for a company's culture through its governance model.

Managing a business based on sound legal principles is essential for success, but far from sufficient. In a fast-changing world, where companies need to optimize their current business while developing a new season, boards have much more pressing tasks than ensuring that financial statements are correct, and the company is compliant.

DEVELOPING THE FUTURE

First, the board needs to make sure that the company has the right strategy and an inspiring dream. The strategy should be focused and translated into a clear direction, a challenging ambition and an engaging inspiration. It is not the board of directors' job to develop the strategy. However, the board must make certain that the right questions are asked in the strategy process. They can help challenge the existing assumptions in the company and inspire new ideas. It can be advantageous if the board has competencies from other industries to add new perspectives. Often, experience from other industries can be a catalyst for spotting a new season and identifying the crucial details.

To help identify a season change, it is relevant for the board to ask the executive team to analyze the overall value chain and evaluate future growth and profitability based on an outside-in approach. This way, the strategic dialogue is focused on the role that the company should play in the future. An analysis of fast-growing new competitors and customers' future needs can also be an inspiration to identify a season change. Work with the strategy should result in an assessment of whether the strategy has been translated into an inspiring dream that has the right direction and ambition.

The most important role of the board of directors is to ensure that the company has the right leadership. Having the right executives in place may be decisive for its ability to reinvent the company. This also applies to coaching teams in sports. A season change sometimes requires an entirely new skillset. The development of the executive team will therefore be crucial for the company and its ability to reinvent.

A continuous evaluation of the composition of the executive team and the division of responsibilities can help ensure a dynamic transition from the old season to the new season. In addition, the composition and focus of the board itself should be continuously adjusted as the company moves to the new season.

DEFINING SUCCESS

Another important task for the board is to decide how the executive team is rewarded. This is not just a question of remuneration, but to a greater extent a decision about how the company defines success. The right executives are typically not motivated by individual items in a bonus plan, but by doing what is right for the company. Nevertheless, a remuneration structure sends a clear message from the board of directors about what it considers important and therefore the remuneration systems becomes an important tool for striking the right balance between the current season and the next and for incorporating the right mindset to accelerate the reinvention.

Traditionally, the executive team is compensated through a combination of a fixed salary and incentives. In most companies, the short term incentives are calculated based on the company's ability to meet the budget agreed for the year. The challenge with this approach is that a bonus based on short-term results focuses attention on the current season, as the existing business is often much more profitable than any investments in the new season. In addition, the model assumes that the future can be planned, which is rarely the case.

In other words, the board has an opportunity to challenge the company's definition of success so that it is more long-term and supports the reinvention. For the Dream and Details leadership model to work, it is critical that the board asks the executives to not only define financial targets, but also performance targets that measure the company's abilities within the crucial details to unlock future opportunities. If this is done correctly, the board will gain insight into how the transformation from the current season to the next season is developing and thus be able to better support management's efforts to reinvent the company. At the same time, the board will be able to better meet shareholders' expectations regarding the company's long-term relevance and value.

Combined with relevant long-term incentives, this creates a balance that is consistent across all stakeholders. A balance that increases the possibilities for a successful reinvention and thus long-term success.

With the right mix of control, risk management and trust, and by asking the right questions, a board of directors can support a company through a process of reinvention. It can support the executive team in taking the right risks, making difficult decisions and help find the right balance between the existing business and the new and thus become a catalyst for reinvention from a position of strength.

Questions that need to be asked about the work in the boardroom are therefore: How much of the board meeting will be spent on the existing business? How much time should be spent on reviewing experimental initiatives that create a next season? Where do we want to take a risk? What have we learned? What details are crucial to the future? What capabilities are needed in the next season? How do we measure our ability to optimize existing business and the ability to perform in a new business? How can we speed up the reinvention process?

In other words, if a season change is likely, the board should refocus its efforts and structure meetings so that the executive team can complete a season change gradually but with accelerating speed. The new season must be supported in the boardroom, where ambitions are set, success is defined, risk is managed, and where a trusting relationship between the board and the executive team sets the tone for a successful reinvention.

CHAPTER 11

LEADERSHIP

In 2017, Fortune magazine named Theo Epstein, President of Baseball Operations for the Chicago Cubs baseball team, the world's best leader – ahead of world-class leaders like Alibaba Group's Jack Ma, Pope Francis, Melinda Gates, Angela Merkel and Jeff Bezos.

The reason for the award was a dream Theo Epstein formulated in 2012: that the Chicago Cubs would win the baseball World Series. At that time, the Cubs had not won the World Series in more than 100 years. They succeeded in 2016, after a series that brought large parts of the United States together to watch the perennial underdogs become champions. As it relates to this book, the most remarkable thing was that the Cubs succeeded by focusing on the development of human potential and values.

Epstein had previously been the general manager for the Boston Red Sox, where he succeeded in bringing a team to the World Series several times and winning the series twice. His approach was in large part based on data analysis, which enabled him to identify the players' personal qualities and their importance to the game.

In 2011, the Boston Red Sox were in the middle of a crisis and fell further and further behind in the standings. Players had conflicts amongst themselves, and the team collapsed when success was no longer within reach. This taught Epstein something important that he brought to Chicago: technical skills and data analysis were not enough. That having strength of character when things are going well does not guarantee strength of character when things go wrong. If the Chicago Cubs were going to win the World Series, they'd have to do it by betting on players who had exceptional character, even in the face of adversity.

During a three-day seminar with other coaches and leaders of the team, Epstein spent the first two days as expected. He talked about his general philosophy for the organization, including the team's game strategy and so on. But the entire last day was dedicated to the human characteristics that Epstein thought were a critical detail. He required his talent scouts to look for more than technically skilled players. They had to provide long reports, based on their own observations and conversations with people close to the players, evaluating the players' personal character traits. Epstein studied the reports, knowing that the character traits were crucial to achieving the dream.

Theo Epstein said flat out that he would win the World Series by basing his leadership on the best human qualities and on the club's ability to put them to play. The latter was as important as the human character in itself. The Cubs needed to focus on the details and development and have a performance mindset that would create the best conditions for players and the team to unleash their potential.

> *"When people do things, they weren't even sure they were capable of, I think it comes back to connection,"* said Theo Epstein in the book The Cubs Way: The Zen of Building the Best Team in Baseball and Breaking the Curse. *"Connection with teammates. Connection with the organization. Feeling like they belong in the environment. I think it's a human need—the need to feel connected. We don't live in isolation. Most people don't like working in isolation—some do, but they typically don't end up playing Major League Baseball."*

When Fortune magazine places a sports executive among the world's top leaders, it tells us that leaders can learn a lot from sports. Epstein himself was less impressed and responded to the award by saying that he couldn't even get his dog to stop peeing on the carpet. "I'm not even the best leader in our organization. It's our players," he said. Epstein's reaction illustrates his approach to leadership. It is about putting others before yourself, and taking responsibility when things don't go well, but giving credit to others for success.

SUCCESSFUL LEADERS IN SPORTS

Sports leaders have always focused on human performance and motivation, both for individuals and teams. The leadership style of successful sports teams has several common features, which have been studied at length. These attributes are also aligned with our leadership philosophy, as they revolve around a dream and crucial details that support leadership as a starting point for future growth.

In the book *Beyond Winning: The Timeless Wisdom of Great Philosopher Coaches*, Gary Walton has identified a number of distinctive features of successful coaches and leaders in the world of sports:

- *They are extremely values-based.*
  Theo Epstein's focus on character traits is an example of values-based leadership that is seen in many of the best sports clubs. Values come first – how they bring home a victory is as important as winning. As applied to Dreams and Details, the values-based focus is the inspirational element of the dream, which runs through a company's mindset and framework.
- *They lead based on a dream with a clear direction and ambition.*
  A common thread that runs through virtually all successes in the sports world is that teams have an unmistakably clear direction. In Dreams and Details, a clear direction, based on the role the company wants to play in the future market, is crucial for the dream to be credible.
- *They set high expectations for performance.*
  In the world of sports, motivation and engagement soars when coaches inspire teams to achieve more than they previously could have imagined. The vast majority of people would feel the same

when they have an opportunity to accomplish something spectacular. It requires a good understanding of the human psyche to hit a level of achievement that is challenging enough to be inspiring, but realistic enough that employees believe in it and don't perceive it as meaningless. In Dreams and Details, the ambition and the work with the details are crucial to this level of performance.

- *They lead individuals with a great focus on the details.*
  On most sports teams, it is typical for coaches to work individually with each player because human performance is crucial. Some players need a lot of support and backing, while others need concrete feedback to be motivated. There is no one-size-fits-all solution. In Dreams and Details, individual leadership is expressed through the micro-leadership on the details, and the framework of the platform must be built to support performance and collaboration.
- *They are consistent and caring.*
  High-performing leaders in the world of sports are able to inspire and motivate individuals while at the same time challenging them when needed. Similarly, employees should not be in doubt about the direction they are headed, and they must be recognized when they perform well, even when the result is below expectations. Leaders need to show that performance is important and is rewarded. Criticism should be constructive and directed forward. Ask: "What can we learn from our mistakes?" rather than "What did we do wrong?"
- *They are honest and have high integrity.*
  Integrity has a lot to do with consistency, but it is also in large part about being credible when communicating internally to the company and with the outside world. You have to be able to rely on a company's leadership team, whether you are an employee, shareholder or business partner. Leaders have to be authentic,

and back their words up with actions that support the dream and show that it is possible to achieve. This is not the same as being charismatic, although that is often considered a must-have trait for leaders. But in fact, research from the CEO Genome Project, which studied thousands of leaders for more than a decade to find patterns and common features, showed that it's not always extroverts who exceed expectations. In other words, do not try to be Steve Jobs if you have a more withdrawn personality. On the other hand, you need to learn to use your true personality to your advantage.

- *They work with the whole person, not just the player.*
  As we described in the chapter about the details, developing performance is dependent upon being a whole and well-functioning person. Therefore, personal development, especially in high-performing environments, is required for professional development. It is absolutely crucial to understand that the person comes first. As leaders, if we do not understand our employees' personality and do not understand how to work with them instead of against them, we risk compromising professional development. As such, we need fewer managers. The American computer pioneer and Navy Rear Admiral Grace Hopper once said, "You manage things. You lead people." When there are people involved, leaders are needed.
- *They are highly competent within their field.*
  Sports leaders typically have a very good understanding of the game. They may not necessarily have been top players, but they know exactly what is required to get the crucial details and they can provide competent feedback. In business, there has been a tendency for the senior executives to be generalists without a specific profession, but to be able to understand and identify the crucial details, you also need a professional background. This does not mean that you must be a civil engineer or programmer

> to work with those teams, but you must have a basic understanding of what needs to be done. The generic idea of good leadership and the supporting functions around it, including HR, measurement tools, schematics and standardized management training, have shifted focus away from specialized professionals. However, in the Dreams and Details mindset, professionals are central. As leaders, if we are going to unfold potential and develop employees, we must be able to draw on our own professional experience.

A final characteristic of successful sports leaders is that they understand the importance of an individual's need for identified meaning-driven motivation and recognition. Without this, players will not see their coaches as the rightful leader. It is ultimately about mutual human respect.

As mentioned earlier, the legendary American football coach Bill Walsh focused primarily on "standards of performance," the philosophy behind his leadership of the San Francisco 49ers. This was his way of removing obstacles and helping his players and team to perform.

> *"I sought to channel the concentration of the 49ers toward improving performance on the field and throughout the organization with as little force as possible from outside influences such as the media, fans, friends or the standings. This was a formidable task, but in large part I accomplished it. The losses hurt, and the wins felt good. But neither was the primary focus of my effort or attention. I knew that if we could keep this focus, winning would take care of itself, and when it didn't I would seek ways to raise our standard of performance. It may not sound very grandiose, but it was very comprehensive and was the platform from which I launched our turnaround."*

GREAT PERFORMANCES HAVE COMMON TRAITS

When considering the leadership qualities above, few doubt that they have a big impact on the world of sports. By consistently training a team's abilities in a specific direction and setting high ambitions, it is possible to realize the dream and produce extraordinary performances. The same applies in the world of art, where realizing a dream and generating singular performances comes from hours of practice and maintaining a high level of professionalism, honesty and consistency.

The reason this leadership philosophy is so crucial to success in sports and the arts is that both disciplines constantly experience season changes. The ability to release human potential is crucial in order to be able to perform in changing seasons.

This is where the dream is key. In his book *Forførelsen (The Seduction)*, Kasper Holten, Director of the Royal Danish Theatre and former Artistic Director of the Royal Danish Opera and former Director of Opera at the Royal Opera House in London, describes the dream as what makes everyone involved move in the same direction and make the right decisions along the way.

> *"The dream in my world is to make people cry. That is to say, our work in the opera requires that we must not only lose ourselves in the production itself, in singing beautifully, in impressing our colleagues, in the subtleties, technicalities, vanities, or anything else, but must also keep the goal in mind: the dream to create performances that move our audience, that evoke new emotions and touch their souls. The opera should act as a 'mental fitness center' for the audience."*

Kasper Holten adds that everything flows from the dream – how to work with the details, the framework and the mindset.

"But the overall principle is for me just to make the dream itself clear to the individual so that every decision they make is guided by the true meaning of it all: to make people cry."

Leaders in sports and art have something else in common with the corporate leadership style of Dreams and Details. Leaders must be very involved when training the crucial details. But when the game or the show starts, the leader's ability to intervene is limited, and that is why it is so important that leaders and coaches train and develop their teams during practices, so that the team can play on its own when it's game day and it finally counts.

In many ways, a conductor of an orchestra conveys the Dreams and Details philosophy. A conductor is responsible for how the orchestra sounds and is experienced. But, a conductor must not make sounds or participate in the performance. A conductor actually has a very limited voice during a concert. A conductor, using only gestures and expressions, must lead the orchestra members individually and as a whole to create a unique experience for the audience. This occurs partly by understanding the role and skills of each musician, and partly by understanding how they collaborate with each other in the orchestra.

But it is also a conductor's responsibility to make sure that everyone has a shared dream of what the music should express and how it should be experienced. The conductor gets everyone on the same sheet of music and ensures that they understand their role in the big picture and have practiced the details to perfection. Without this, music might be made, but nothing more. With the right dream, in which musicians can develop individually and together to their full potential, magic is created.

Throughout this book, we have argued that business environments are increasingly similar to sports, art and science, where conditions change from season to season and from game to game. But even if there is no season change, most successful leaders – regardless of the world they come from – understand that focusing on developing people and unleashing their potential creates the best performances.

The leadership think tank High Performance Institute, with which we are affiliated, conducted a study with a group of successful leaders over a period of five years starting in 2005. The goal was to determine whether there were common leadership traits that gave the best performance in business, the world of sports, art and science. The results showed that, while they worked under widely different conditions, three primary traits were at the core of their success: persistence, perfection and innovation. It applied wherever they came from, and from this work, the institute developed nine recommendations for exceptional leadership:

- Create meaning and passion.
- Ensure that development and performance take place in parallel.
- Develop talent and unleash potential.
- Bet on specialists.
- Dare to pick the team - and cut it as needed.
- Provide specific and acknowledging feedback.
- Praise often and genuinely.
- Create a team culture, also for the individual.
- Use your intuition as an important part of judgment

The above recommendations, echoed by Theo Epstein, Gary Walton and Bill Walsh, are surprisingly in line with what Robert K. Greenleaf introduced back in the 1970's as "Servant Leadership." Supported by James C. Hunter in the book *The Servant*, a servant leader has the following characteristics:

- Possesses the will and desire to lead and help others.

- Provides loving attention in the service of the cause.
- Serves and sacrifices so others can succeed.
- Appears as an authority in the eyes of others.
- Leads through earned influence.

The right of leadership is replaced by the duty of leadership, and the power to force people to do something is replaced by making people want to follow the leader.

As former commander of several international military operations, including a major operation to challenge insurgents in the Helmand Province in Afghanistan, the Danish colonel and now Master of Ceremonies (COO) at The Royal Danish Court, Kim Kristensen, states it in his book Follow Me:

> *"Servant Leadership is that you have to care for and love your soldiers. Understood in the following way that you should be patient, caring, humble, respectful and forgiving in your leadership behavior. Because you must remember that the soldiers are not there for the officers. It is the other way around. The officers are there for the soldiers. You can never pay them to follow you through a crossfire, they need to follow you for totally different reasons."*

With that in mind a high performance leader following the Dreams and Details leadership model is a "Servant Leader" and not a "Self-Serving Leader." The leader works in the company's and employees' service – they are not tools for achieving the leader's personal ambition.

The rationale behind Dreams and Details is largely about ensuring that the mentioned leadership principles come more into play in business. We believe that it is relevant for business leaders to be inspired by the leadership required to perform at high level in art and sports. We are convinced that, just like in the world of sports and art, human qualities will be competitive differentiators in companies in a digital future, where the ability to transform and reinvent defines future winners.

LEADING WITH DREAMS AND DETAILS

The Dreams and Details leadership model requires that leaders are able to lead a company's existing business and develop new businesses in parallel. Leading people in accordance with Dreams and Details is simply about helping them perform at a higher level – helping them become the best possible version of themselves – helping them beat their best. It is about earning the company's trust and the respect of your employees, which is no easy task. It defines new requirements for transformational leadership.

Of course, it is not possible to develop a leadership style that can be implemented and work in all organizations. However, transformational leadership stays the same: defining an inspiring dream, leading the change of the crucial details and implementing the platform for change. This applies to everyone, regardless of where the leader is located in an organization. This applies to the board of directors, the executive board and team leaders.

In the future, we believe leaders will work together as a team that operates both horizontally and vertically in a dynamic collaboration internally and with others outside the company – like a network. They must have insight, understanding and respect for each other's leadership, because they are dependent on each other to make the company succeed.

Leadership will evolve as the company reinvents itself. It is the leaders' responsibility and privilege to reinvent the company and their own leadership style to accomplish this. If successful, the right leadership can motivate people to perform far beyond what they themselves thought possible.

This is important because leadership today goes far beyond optimizing business results and reinventing the business itself. In a global and interconnected world with increasing uncertainty and deep transformational changes, business leaders play an important role in contributing to progress in society.

The founder of the World Economic Forum, Klaus Schwab, defined responsive and responsible leadership this way:

> *"Taking the right decisions in a complex world that suffers from legacy issues and emotional turmoil is the daunting task of today's leaders. To fulfil this task, leaders need sensitivity to serve as their radar system, and values and vision as their compass. Without a radar system, there can be no acceptability; and without a compass, there can be no credibility. Ultimately, we are measured on the basis of our values, vision and actions. Leadership today can no longer be built on privilege, but only on sustained and sincere efforts to earn trust. Only leaders who clearly distinguish themselves by transcending their own interests and serving those of society warrant being considered elite."*

Thus, leadership means – more than ever – taking responsibility and demonstrating courage and commitment to honestly explain the breadth and complexity of issues, proactively generate solutions and take action on what we stand for.

EPILOGUE – A NEW SEASON FOR LEADERSHIP?

In 2008, the CEO of SAP Henning Kagermann offered me an opportunity to develop my leadership skills in order to prepare me for a more global role in the company. I was invited to join the Avira Quest program at INSEAD. After a week of theoretical education focused on the role of business in globalization at INSEAD, we went on a fieldtrip to India to experience globalization in reality. The program was designed by Professor Subramanian Rangan from INSEAD in cooperation with an organization called Leaders Quest, founded by Lindsay Levin. In many ways, the program fundamentally changed my view on leadership.

On the trip, we met a number of local leaders. Some were politicians, some were business people and others came from social organizations and grassroots movements. Their backgrounds were very diverse, as were the businesses, challenges and opportunities they represented. But even though we met leaders from large, successful companies, it was the young Indian NGO-leader Devika Mahadevan who made the biggest impression on me.

Mumbai is chaotic. A megacity with at least 20 million people crammed together, and more coming every day. The need for new buildings and a new infrastructure is huge. More than 35 million people are employed in the construction industry in India, with a large part of them in Mumbai. In most cases, whole families live with the workers on construction sites, as they have no other choice. When the construction work is over, the family moves on to the next construction site. This constant movement to new locations makes it impossible for the children to go to school, limiting their possibilities later in life and creating major social problems.

When we met Devika Mahadevan in 2008, more than 40,000 children lived on construction sites. Devika was director of Mumbai Mobile Creches, which works on solving the problem by creating temporary schools on actual construction sites. The schools moved into the buildings under construction as soon as there was a roof on the ground floor. Devika explained to us how the Mumbai Mobile Creches recruited teachers for the schools among older well-educated women in the neighborhood who wanted to teach the children for a few hours every day.

Sponsors helped with materials and administration, and that is how Mumbai Mobile Creches was able to give the children an education and a better chance in life than their parents had.

Devika's dream was concrete and very inspiring: "10,000 by 10," she called it. She wanted to educate 10,000 children a year by 2010. Devika had taken over the role as director from her grandmother, who started the organization back in 1969. The "10 x 10" dream, as it was later called, became the foundation for the NGO's growth and created opportunities for fundraising. Today it has put more than 100,000 children on 270 construction sites in school, while more than 1,000 adults have become educated as teachers.

Devika's story is a good example on how a clear vision and strong authentic leadership can solve even the most hopeless situations in the world. Devika did not lead a large organization with many employees. In fact, most involved were volunteers inspired by her dream. She didn't have a large budget, nor did she earn a lot of money. The basic idea of her concept was to ensure solid education for the children in need. The cost per child was less than $20 per month. Despite being a small organization with a limited budget, Devika created opportunities for many people and created future dreams for many children in Mumbai through her personal leadership of Mumbai Mobile Creches.

Even though Devika was only 30 years old, she had in many ways already understood what leadership is all about: engaging and creating a community working to achieve a dream and unleashing human potential.

Often, we assume that the size or importance of your leadership is measured by the size of the organization or budget you are in charge of. Devika showed that leadership is about the difference you can make, motivating others to commit to the dream of the organization, and your ability to engage and develop people, even if they are volunteers.

Traditional leadership is largely based on the power that the title or role gives the leader. Traditional leadership is therefore focused on using the assigned power to ensure that the organization or employees implement the decisions made by management. Devika Mahadevan's example shows that you don't need any formal power to lead people towards a shared dream and achieve significant impact. It is the dream, the passion and your authentic leadership that makes the difference.

Leadership that benefits from the Dreams and Details leadership model is different from power-based leadership. It is leadership based on the ability to inspire people to develop and use their full potential to pursue a shared dream. It is leadership based on the influence you can have on other people and on the ability to unleash human potential and develop collaboration between them. It is about unleashing creativity and creating room to find new and better opportunities.

We often associate competent leadership with the ability to define goals and make decisions, and subsequently ensure that the decisions are executed, and performance goals met. That form of leadership works well in organizations where you have the formal power over all involved and in situations where it is possible to plan the future, make correct decisions based on facts and implement the decisions according to existing assumptions.

In a period of frequent season changes, it is difficult to obtain all the knowledge necessary to make the right decisions, and it is often impossible to create an optimal plan since the conditions are unknown. The plans and targets will often prove to be too conservative or too ambitious depending on where you are on the exponential curve. In this context, traditional leadership models have a great risk of limiting performance and outcomes to what was planned. This will only reduce inspiration, courage and the will to pursue bigger dreams.

To use the ideas in this book about leading organizations and people towards a common dream and unlocking the full potential in the crucial details, it is necessary to start with your own leadership style and your own assumptions about your role as a leader. The type of leadership that benefits from our thinking is not based on the power to decide, control of plans and measuring results. Rather, Dreams and Details leadership is about the ability to create clarity, trust and consequences, and using your influence to inspire others to follow a dream, and develop their potential.

Transformation and change starts with clarity. If the dream is unclear, it is difficult to inspire everyone. Clarity around the details is also crucial, as the choice of details focuses the organization on where to make significant changes happen. Clarity in selecting what details not to focus on is equally important to the organization's ability to concentrate on the details that matter the most. Finally, clarity around the mindset and framework increases the credibility of the dream and builds a platform for change. This creates room for people to develop individually and in collaboration with each other.

Instead of focusing on making the right decisions based on a firm business plan, leadership is largely about increasing the organization's ability to optimally handle any situation that comes their way. Clarity about the dream, the details and the platform create the foundation for engagement among everyone involved and increases an organization's ability to make decisions when needed. The Dreams and Details leadership model is not about having the right answers, but about asking the right questions to the right people at the right time. It is about creating a mindset and a framework that ensures that employees have the opportunity to make the right decisions themselves.

"Confidence is good, control is better." We often use this argument, when we introduce control systems to ensure implementation of our plans. But what if that is not right? We assert that control of predefined plans limits an organization's ability to reinvent itself. By controlling the implementation of a predefined plan, you accomplish, at best, a path that is implemented as planned. But what if it turns out that the plan is becoming irrelevant and is therefore not the optimal plan anymore? In most cases the plan is limited by the knowledge and assumptions available at the time when the plan was created.

During a season change, the plan is most likely wrong, as conditions change along the way, and are unknown from the beginning. Instead of controlling that everything goes as planned, the type of leadership described in this book puts a high degree of trust in people and their ability to find a better path and to develop exponentially as individuals and as teams.

Trust is as important as clarity. Trust-based leadership believes in people's potential and the synergy in their collaboration when they are inspired by the same dream and willing to practice the crucial details to perfection. There are many examples of people being able to move mountains, figuratively, when they are driven by an inspiring dream. Money and titles rarely move mountains, but commitment, will and abilities do.

Leadership changes radically when it is based on trust. Leadership based on trust assumes that people, engaged in the dream with the will to develop the crucial details, can unfold their full potential better than in a control-based system. Leadership based on trust requires that you, as a leader, are willing to listen and learn. In addition, it is important to recognize and manage mistakes, so they can become learning opportunities for the organization.

Trust is not something you acquire; it is something you earn over time. Trust is based on who we are and the way we do things. Trust also builds on the honesty of recognizing weakness and mistakes as well as taking the responsibility and be firm when necessary. To create trust-based leadership, you also have to be able to set aside individual objectives and remove political and bureaucratic agendas in the organization. Trust goes both ways. It is a mutual commitment between leaders and employees.

Finally, leadership requires consistency and an uncompromising adherence to principles and priorities. Without these qualities, the vision becomes blurred and the transformation is weakened. True reinvention can only occur by consistently and uncompromisingly holding yourself and everyone around you to a higher standard and adhering to the principles that support your dream.

Many perceive leadership based on trust as weak, but in reality, it can be very consistent and strong. An uncompromising leader who gives and receives trust can produce greater results than a leader who is merely obeyed due to their position of power.

In control-based leadership, individual employees are often evaluated annually to judge their ability to achieve predetermined goals. Employees who exceed their goals will get a good evaluation, often with a higher bonus. Employees who do not reach their goals receive a poor evaluation and no bonus. The system is relative and does not always ensure the right or meaningful evaluation of performance. The employees who did not reach their goals could have performed better than anyone expected under the circumstances and vice versa. In addition, the system does not necessarily develop employees' capabilities and performance on the crucial details.

Uncompromising leadership based on trust is much more binary. When the leader assesses an employee, it is from an either/or standpoint: either the employee has the will to engage in the dream and the ability to develop his or her potential in relation to the crucial details – or not. If not, an uncompromising leader will move the person into a different setting or role. An uncompromising leader gives everyone a chance to develop their potential for achieving the dream but must hold people accountable who do not want to or cannot develop.

The same applies to the principles and values in the organization. As a leader, you cannot accept a break with fundamental principles or values, not even from the most valuable employees or leaders. Of course, this also applies to oneself. Similarly, you cannot accept disloyal behaviors, unfair treatment of others or political games – especially not among the leaders in the organization. Disloyalty in relation to the dream or the team requires uncompromising action. Uncompromising leadership will increase clarity and trust in the organization and unite the organization as they work to reach the dream. One could describe it as an uncompromising and caring act for both the organization and its employees.

Traditional leadership is based on objective knowledge and facts. Objective knowledge is of course necessary to make logical decisions. But in a season change, the challenge is that you often don't have enough objective knowledge or facts to make the right decisions. Instead of postponing the decision to a point where sufficient knowledge is available, leadership in a season change is about managing experience-based intuitive knowledge, and a realistic assessment of what isn't known yet. We must dare to use our judgement.

Perhaps one of the most important characteristics of the leadership style we are recommending is to have courage. Courage to acknowledge facts, even if the facts go against your assumptions. Courage to trust your own intuition. Courage to trust others. Courage to dare to experiment with something unknown. Courage to acknowledge your own mistakes and learn from them. Courage to be honest. Courage to be uncompromising. Courage to be authentic by infusing leadership with your personality. And above all, courage to challenge your own assumptions and develop and lead in a world that requires constant reinvention.

As always, change starts from within. We hope Dreams and Details gives you inspiration and courage to reinvent your own role as a leader so you can lead the reinvention of your business from a position of strength.

THANK YOU

When we decided to write a book about leadership it was based on a shared dream to find a solution to one of the most demanding leadership challenges: How do you lead a successful reinvent of an organization from a position of strength? How do you inspire people to change when they are successful, so they can perform at an even higher level? How do you overcome the "innovators dilemma" that prevent many successful companies from reinventing themselves in times of radical change?

We didn't have the answer when we started our dialog, but we knew that the answer was based on the ability to unleash human potential.

This book was created through numerous discussions, analysis, reflections and ideas. The Dreams and Details leadership model is a result of many iterations. The core of the leadership model was always about how to develop human potential. The leadership model was developed from this core and became clearer every time we met, as new inspiration, examples and experiences defined each of the elements of the leadership model.

Bringing the dreams and the details of the leadership model together in a consistent way was the biggest challenge. We are grateful for the support and perseverance of Susanne Sayers, who helped translate our thoughts from ideas in our mind to words on paper. Thank you for your courage, lovely character and belief that this book needed to be written.

Also a big thanks to Rikke and Bill Fryman for their support and patience in translating the book from Danish to English. Thank you for helping us reinvent the book once again.

Mikael Trolle & Jim Hagemann Snabe

ABOUT THE AUTHORS

Jim Hagemann Snabe is Chairman of A.P. Møller – Maersk A/S (DK) and Siemens AG (D). He is Vice Chairman of Allianz SE (D) and a Member of the Board of Trustees at World Economic Forum. Jim has developed his career through 24 years of service in the IT industry. Throughout his career Jim has had leadership roles at SAP and IBM, leading global consulting-, sales- and product development organizations. He was appointed member of the Executive Board Member of SAP in 2008 and co-CEO of SAP AG in 2010 alongside Bill McDermott. Through his involvement with the World Economic Forum Jim is actively engaged in efforts related to the digital transformation of business and society. Jim Hagemann Snabe has a M.Sc. (Economics and Business Administration) from Aarhus University and is adjunct professor at Copenhagen Business School, CBS.

Mikael Trolle is the CEO and Partner of the Dreams and Details Academy. For 28 years, he was CEO and Sports Director in Volleyball Denmark and for two periods, the head coach of the men's national volleyball team. Mikael's career has spanned eight years as an international volleyball player, followed by 21 years in head coaching positions at club and international level summing up 342 matches spearheading the men's national team. He is a a lecturer and examiner at the University of Copenhagen and at Copenhagen Business School Executive's High Performance Leadership programs. Mikael is as well a speaker at the High Performance Institute. As a consultant and corporate advisor, he has worked with numerous Danish and International companies and organizations, such as Novo Nordisk, The Danish Government, The Royal Danish Theater and the Danish Broadcasting Corporation DR. Mikael holds an M.Sc. in Biology and Sports Science from the University of Copenhagen.

LITERATURE

In our search for leadership to reinvent organizations from a position of strength, we have been inspired by experiences, stories and reflections from great leaders from the worlds of business, sports and art. Here is a collection of the books that have inspired us most.

BOOKS

Anderson, Chris: *The Long Tail*, Hyperion Books, 2006.

Biswas-Diener, Robert and Ben Dean: *Positive Psychology Coaching – Putting the Science of Happiness to Work for Your Clients*, Wiley & Sons, 2007.

Boynton, Andy and Bill Fischer: *Virtuoso Teams – Lessons From Teams That Changed the World*, Prentice Hall, 2005.

Buckingham, Marcus and Curt Coffman: *First, Break all The Rules*, Simon & Schuster 1999.

Bungay, Stephen: *The Art of Action*, Nicholas Brealey Publishing, 2010.

Christensen, Clayton: *The Innovator's Dilemma*, Collins Business Essentials, 1997.

Collins, Jim: *Good to Great*, Cornerstone, 2001.

Collins, Jim: *How The Mighty Fall*, HarperCollins Publishers, 2009.

Colvin, Geoff: *Talent is Overrated*, Nicholas Brealey Publishing, 2008.

Coyle, Daniel: *The Talent Code – Greatness isn't born, it's grown*, Random House Books, 2009.

Csikszentmihalyi, Mihaly and Susan A. Jackson: *Flow in Sports*, Human Kinetics, 1999.

Deci, Edward L. and Richard M Ryan.: *Intrinsic Motivation and Self-Determination Theory in Human Behavior*, Plenum Press, 1985.

Deci, Edward L. and Richard Flaste: *Why We Do What We Do – Understanding Self-Motivation*, Penguin Books, 1995.

Delehanty, Hugh and Phil Jackson: *Sacred Hoops*, Hyperion, 1995

Dweck, Carol S.: *Mindset: How You Can Fulfil Your Potential*, Robinson, 2000.

Dweck, Carol S.: *Self-theories: Their Role in Motivation, Personality, and Development*, Psychology Press, 2000.

Friedman, Thomas: *The World is Flat*, Penguin Books Ltd., 2007.

Godin, Seth: Purple Cow: *Transform Your Business by Being Remarkable*, Penguin, 2007.

Gothelf, Jeff and Josh Seiden: *Sense & Respond*, Harvard Business Review Press, 2017.

Greenleaf, Robert K: *The Servant as Leader*, Greenleaf Center, 1970/1991.

Grove, Andrew S.: *Only the Paranoid Survive*, Profile Business, 1996.

Hamel, Gary and C.K. Prahalad: *Competing for the Future*, Harvard Business School Press, 1994.

Hamel, Gary: *Leading the Revolution*, Harvard Business School Press, 2000.

Hamel, Gary and Bill Breen: *The Future of Management*, Harvard Business School Press, 2007.

Hamel, Gary: *The Future of Management*, Harvard Business School Press, 2007.

Hamel, Gary: *What Matters Now*, Jossey-Bass/Wiley, 2012.

Handy, Charles: *The Second Curve*, Random House Books, 2015.

Hood, Christopher: *A Government That Worked Better and Cost Less*, Oxford University Press, 2015.

Hunter, James C.: *The Servant*, Crown Business, 2008.

Isaacson, Walter: *Steve Jobs*, Gyldendal, 2011.

Jameson, Steve: *Bill Walsh' winning Ways*, New Word City, 2011.

Jamieson, Steve: *Wooden on Leadership – How to create a winning organization*, McGraw-Hill, 2005

Jaworski, Joseph: *Synchronicity*, Berret-Koehler Publishers Inc., 1996.

Kegan, Robert and Lisa Laskow Lahey: *An Everyone Culture*, Harvard Business Review Press, 2016.

Kristensen, Kim: *Follow Me - Leading From The Front*, Maverick House, 2017.

Kolind, Lars and Jacob Bøtter: *Unboss*, Jyllandspostens Forlag, 2012.

Leinwand, Paul, Cesare Mainardi and Art Kleiner: *Strategy That Works*, Harvard Business Review Press, 2016.

Levann, Allan and Mikael Trolle: *Den store præstation (The Significant Performance)*, Gyldendal Business, 2010. (only available in Danish).

Malmgren, Philippa: *Signals – How everyday sign can help us navigate the world's turbulent economy*. Orion Publishing Group Limited, 2016.

McGrath, Rita Gunther: *The End of Competitive Advantage*, Harvard Business Review Press, 2013.

Pink, Daniel: Drive: *The Surprising Truth About What Motivates Us*, Riverhead Books, 2011.

Reeves, Martin, Knut Haanæs and Janmejaya Sinha: *Your Strategy Needs a Strategy*, Harvard Business Review Press, 2015.

Schwab, Klaus: *The Fourth Industrial Revolution*, World Economic Forum, 2016.

Sheldon, Kennon: *Motivation*, CAPP Press, 2008.

Schön, Donald A.: *The Reflective Practitioner – How Professionals Think in Action*, Harper Collins Publisher. 1983

Simonton, Dean Keith: *Behavioral and Brain Sciences: Defining and finding talent*, Cambridge University Press, 1998.

Sinek, Simon: *Start With Why*, Portfolio/Penguin, 2007.

Stone, Brad: *Amazon.com –The Everything Store: Jeff Bezos ans Age of Amazon*, Hachette Group, 2013.

Tanggaard, Lene and Malene Friis Andersen: *Tæller vi det der tæller? – målstyring og standardisering i arbejdslivet (Do we count what counts? - Result management and standardization in business and organizations)*, Klim, 2016. (only available in Danish).

Tobin, Jack: *They call me coach*, McGraw-Hill, 2004

Trolle, Mikael and Peter Brüchmann: *Sportens største ledere – Hemmeligheden bag store præstationer (Great leader in sports – The secret behind their extraordinary performance)*, Gyldendal Business, 2014. (only available in Danish).

Verducci, Tom: *The Cubs Way – The Zen of Building the Best Team in Baseball and Breaking the Curse (Theo Epstein)*, Crown Publishing Group, 2017.

Walsh, Craig og Steve Jamison: *The Score Takes Care of Itself (Bill Walsh)*, Portfolio Publishers, 2009.

Walton, Gary: *Beyond Winning – The Timeless Wisdom of Great Philosopher Coaches*, Harpers Press, 1992.

Zander, Benjamin and Rosamund Stone Zander: *The Art of Possibility*, Penguin, 2000.

RESEARCH AND CASESTUDIES

Cranet report, 2016: Human Resource Management and Performance Management. Research project about the value of outcomes measures, 1991-2014.

Harter, James K. and Frank L. Schmidt, Emily A. Killham, James W. Asplund: *Q12 Meta-Analysis.* Gallup Inc. 2006.

Garvin, David A., and Carin-Isabel Knoop: "The National Geographic Society (A)." Harvard Business School Case 311-002, January 2011. (Edited November 2015).

INDEX

I

J

K

L

M

N

P

R

S

T

W

Z

Printed in Great Britain
by Amazon

63598373R00147